Brummagem Bill

For Doris, my wife & soul mate. xxx

Brummagem Bill

Brummagem Bill

Printed August 2010

Prologue

My Dad died in July 1960. It was quite a shock to us all owing to the fact that he never had any illness in his life. He just came down from the garden to have his tea, he sat at the table and he had a fall off the chair. My Mother was in the other room, she heard him fall, went in to him and he was dead on the floor. She called our neighbour in to help her but he said he was dead. The Doctor came in and certified the death, when the post mortem was done it was confirmed cerebral haemorrhage. He was just 60 years of age.

His Mother, who was alive at the time, told us his father died of the same thing. He died in Birmingham town centre; he was 57 years of age.

I had passed the house the day my Dad had died. I was so much in a hurry to get home. We had gone to bed the on the night and about midnight there was a knock at the door. It was a mate come up and he said "did you get the message Bill?" I said "What message?" he said "your Dad has died". My brother had phoned The Bell pub in Northfield and left the message, so I drove over to my Mother's house, my two brothers had gone over to my house – we must have passed each other.

Brummagem Bill

My Dad was cremated at Perry Barr crematorium. His ashes are buried at the top of his garden with roses all around it. He lived for his garden. All his spare cash and time was spent on his garden.

Christmas was getting near and I said to my Mother "would you like to come and spend Christmas with us?" she said "you are the first to ask so I will come to yours". She came a couple of days before and said "What are we having for Christmas dinner?", I said "Just a minute" and I went outside and brought in two live cockerels, I said "take your pick Mum", we all had a good laugh but dirty looks from the cockerels.

After a few years of living on her own she wanted to move to another house, she said every time she went in to the kitchen her eyes kept focussing on the kitchen floor where my Dad had died. She told me she could see the floor breathing, it was playing on her mind. She had several moves, one of them near my sister's house. Eventually she got a place back at Kingstanding but her health was deteriorating.

She went in to a nursing home on College Road and from there to Dudley Road Hospital where she died on the 4th May 1987 at the age of 90 years. She was cremated at Perry Barr crematorium.

Brummagem Bill

Brummagem Bill

The biggest shock of losing someone is when you lose one of your children. You don't expect them to go before you but that did happen to us, our eldest son Billy. Doris and I were at home on a miserable snowy night in February 1991.

Doris's sister and her husband come up to the house, I opened the door and I said to both of them "You picked a nice night to come and visit us". They come in and said "there's no nice way to say this, your Billy's dead". I just screamed out, we cried our eyes out. Valerie had phoned Mary and broke the bad news and asked them to come up and tell us, they lived minutes away, as she was too upset to tell us. He was just 41 years of age. He was music mad. I took him up town to buy his first electric guitar, he was so proud of it. I said to him the day we got it I would pay for him to have lessons; they said at the shop we got it from that they did this. But he said no, his mates that lived nearby would help and teach him. He liked reggae music, Jimmy Hendrix, Bob Marley stuff and he was a big fan of the Rolling Stones. When Mick Jagger was on TV I used to imitate him and he used to do his nut (happy days.)

They will never come back..... Just the memories (and thank God for them).

Brummagem Bill

Chapter One

My father's name was Arthur James Cornelius Wintle. My mother's name was Emily Harriet Wintle nee Whitehouse.

I was one of five children, the eldest being Arthur, he was born in 1920 Clifton Road, Sparkbrook, Birmingham. Elsie was born in an attic on Litchfield Road in 1922, Aston. Syd was next, he was born in 1924, at 219 Dartmouth Street Aston and my self Bill in 1928 and Fred was born at the same address in 1930.

The house was one of Rudders and Payne's, they were timber haulers. My father worked there, he drove a team of horses for the firm collecting trees and delivering timber. My Dad's uncle also worked there. He got a medal from the R.S.P.C.A for saving some horses at the big fire in November 1937.

My father was brought up by his mother's parents in Cheltenham; they were Haines of Cheltenham, also timber haulers. None of their lads went to school. My great Uncle Syd said my Dad could drive a team of horses as good as any man at the age of ten years of age.

However, the men could measure the length and girth by sight and they could tell you what sizes of timber you could be cut out of it, 4 by 2, 3 by 2 and so on.

On my Dad's side of the, family the Wintle's; they came from

Brummagem Bill

Longhope and Taynton in Gloucester. They have been farming round since C1500 and are still farming at Taynton and on the A48 there is a Wintle's Hill going down to Weston on Severn, Gloucester.

After my brother was born in 1930, my parents got a house at 28 Sidcup Road, Kingstanding. It was a new house on a new council estate. There was a school near by; the senior was still having work done to it so my eldest brother had to go on a bus to school not far away until it was finished. I went to the infants; our new head teacher was a Miss Boot. I went through my schooling there apart from the time I was evacuated during the Second World War.

My mother would do washing for her mother, she would push a pram with my brother in it and I would walk at the side of the pram from Sidcup Road to Lichfield Road Aston, and the route we would take was cutting across our estate to the Ridgeway down to the Brookvale Road and alongside the river Tame, down Tame Road and cutting across Lichfield to our Gran's Coffee House. It was always dark curtains on the doors, plants in the windows, a chenille table cloth. She had a glass dome with fruit in it, I would have liked a pear but I found out they was artificial. They had a glass cabinet full of stuffed birds on display in a natural wildlife surrounding with heather and stone and rocks in their bedroom. When my Gran died my mother's eldest brother, Uncle George, he had fits, came to live with us. He had nowhere to go. He had quite a few fits with us; he got pneumonia and went in to Dudley Road Hospital where he died.

When my mother come back from the hospital she gave me my Uncle's pocket watch and told me to look after it. I was only young at the time and it did not take long before I had the back off as kids do. My Mother should have saved it 'til I was much older.

We would go to the back of the house that led onto Wainwright street where there was a little pub called "The Manor', my Gran used to sit on a little stool just inside and have a drink, me and my brother would play hide and seek, sometimes she would hide our faces in her long black frock. We used to float match boxes in the horse trough opposite the pub till the horse came up for a drink, these horse troughs were all over the place – road haulage was mainly by horses, your milk, bread, coal and heavy goods and so on.. And any heavy loads or hills to climb they would take an extra horse tied at the back of the dray or cart and they would bring him or her to the front to help to get up the hill. I have seen this happen on numerous occasions. Kingston hill was one where there was a horse trough at the top by the pub, The Greenway, at the fork of Cattal and Coventry road, and a much earned drink was always welcomed by the horses and probably by the Carters as well - in the pub!!

My Grandmothers place was at 79 Lichfield Road; Aston, It was a Coffee House, I think and that was where my dad met my mother, just after the First World War.

When we had the bad winters and loads of snow, the carters would wrap sacking around the horse's feet to help them to move better. There were also metal studs they used to screw into the existing shoes to grip in the snow and ice. Mom would get the washing packed and ready to take back. My uncle Joe kept pigeons here "Tumblers" I was so fascinated by them, I had some later on myself! They also had a big dog in a cage run – Airedale cross I think it was and not very friendly. My Uncle's – Mom's brothers Joe and Albert used to make Cigarettes on a machine, they would put the tobacco in, some papers in another part of the machine and turn a handle and out came the cigarettes. They would pass them through a small window into the Cafe where they would be sold loose. It was a thing they did in those days. We never went into the cafes side of it, we always used the back part of the house, and our Mom would then take us back to Kingstanding.

Brummagem Bill

There used to be a large blue cup and saucer that stood in the cafe at my grandmother's place. My mother had it, and when she died I had it – it's in the glass cabinet that my mom used to have. It will stay there until I "pop my clogs".   .

When we was kids our mom used to take me and Fred picking potatoes down old oscott hill she would get a few pence from the farmer and bring a few back for tea we went with our neighbours.

In 1936 when King George VI became king my mother organized a coronation party in Sidcup road and made outfits for us all. She made me up as king and one of our neighbour's daughters as queen. Agnes hope. We all had a good party we got our piano out in the road – we all had coronation mugs, tins of chocolate for the occasion some people had other types of gifts, one young lad was given a penknife with the kings head on it. He opened it up – brought it down on my wrist and cut it. I still have the scar today. So I was crowned and almost assassinated on the same day ....God Save the King!

During the school holidays my mother would organise trips out for the school children; she would book a charabang to Evesham, we would get on the pleasure steamer and go down the river for a few miles, come back and have tea at the cafe – then back home. Some parents would come to help with the children. She would organise evening mystery trips for the adults to places like Holffleet and Bewdley etc...

Chapter Two

I was eleven when world war two broke out; there were no televisions just wireless radios. We all had to keep quiet when the Prime Minister Neville Chamberlain made his speech. For the next few weeks people were digging holes in their back gardens. A few weeks later the Anderson shelters started to arrive they were dropped on the pavement outside your house with a bag of nuts and bolts and instructions. So it was all actions till it was up. The bombing raids was soon to come, soon whenever we were to hear the sirens we would get up and go down the shelter till the all clear was sounded then go back to our own bed. From where we lived you could see across towards town and the sky would be lit up. We had an Aunt and Uncle living in Barton St; Aston — Back of the Aston Hippodrome.

My two cousins Lilly and Leonard come to live with us because of the bombings there. We used to go to school in the morning, looking for pieces of shrapnel on the ground to collect. The cousins stayed with us till we were evacuated to Derby, Fred and I went to Sommercotes, it was on a redundant farm house, with plenty of farm buildings — but nothing inside. A kid's paradise! Well it was for us!

A nice orchard just outside our front door, our toilet was next to two pig sty's I can see the logic in that! It was a wooden box with a hole in it, a metal round tin underneath - the council would come and empty it on the night the farmer told them to empty it on his land and he would plough it in. The people that we stayed with were a Mr and Mrs Whetton. They had a son named Gordon, he was 5 years old. We called them Aunt Madge and Uncle George. He was a coal miner on nights, our bathing facilities was a tub that you stood in. The school we went to was Birchwood Lane, Sommercotes, an old chapel divided into two classrooms and our teachers were from Peckam Road School, we could hear both lessons at the same time.

In the next field was a working farm owned by Mr & Mrs Bryan — we used to get our milk off Mr Clifford, he had a horse and cart with milk churns in. They would measure the pints and pour it in our jug. I used to like to drink off some of the cream if no one was looking. Occasionally my brother Fred and I would go down to the farm to get the milk; they would probably still be milking. We would look on and Mr Bryan would turn the cow's teat on to our face and squirt it onto us.

I used to call the cows a camouflaged herd. I went back many years later before he died and he said "Bill – there's your camouflaged herd over there" He had still remembered. I can still see his face now after all these years. He has a son and when I was driving over to Derby I thought that I would pop in to see him. I drove down to the farm that we were evacuated to and to my great disappointment the cottage was there but all the other buildings had been knocked down, there was a tractor in the field and a chap got out and started to walk over towards me with a grin on his face.

I said "Hello Mr Bryan" he had not changed at all – his one shoulder dropped as he got near, he remembered me and told me that his dad had died a few years ago. I said to him "Your dad will never be dead as long as you are alive – you are the spitting image of him" he said "Come over and meet Mom and my wife" I went to meet them and had a nice cup of tea and a slice of cake. When I was leaving he said take some potatoes back with you and he gave me two bags. I said "can I have a quick look around the sheds?" He said "Yes, come on" and took me to the cow sheds where they used to milk the cows. I told him, what his dad used to do, He said "he's done it to all of us kids".

Brummagem Bill

In the lane there used to be a shop called "Cockains" – or something similar they sold homemade jams and pickles the smell from the shop was lovely a few doors farther on down was a house where one of my school friends Reg Markland lived, he used to get the coal in for his neighbours, they got free coal if their husbands were coal miners, they used to drop it outside their houses on the pavement.

He got a few bob for doing that. There was another mate Harold Cornfield, he lived at Rose Cottage in Sleetmore Lane, he wasn't very happy there, he said one of the family used to lick his plate and it made him feel sick. So I asked our aunt and uncle if he could come and live with us they said yes so we spoke to the billeting officer the next day and they said he could so he moved in.

Another pal of mine was a Frank Williams he and his sister came to Derby with us – he came up to the farm from time to time. We used to collect birds eggs, if there was five in the nest you could take one but that's against the law today. There used to be a taxidermist on the corner of Suffolk Street and Navigation Street in Birmingham who sold birds eggs of all kinds. In the corner shop there was a big bear, stuffed birds, stouts and squirrels around the shop, and when you went in he would step from behind the bear from another room.

We bought eggs from time to time. I was about ten years of age and felt very scared of the bear as it looked so real. When we came out of the shop we kept looking around to make sure he wasn't following us!

On Christmas our Aunt Madge asked us what we would like for Christmas my brother said he would like a rabbit. I had a pair of fantail pigeons. Our Mom & Dad came over and brought some clothes, boots, Wellingtons a football etc. so we was set up for the winter. Uncle George took us to see his parents in Westhouses; Alfretton on Boxing Day. Christmas day soon went, the Snow Drops were popping up in the orchard - it was a lovely sight – a sight I will always remember. Every time I see snow drops in the fields along the side of the roads my mind goes back to the Corner House farm Sleetmore lane, Sommercotes Derbyshire. A memory I will always treasure. Christmas school holidays were over and I think it was this time that Gordon Whetton was starting school. I used to carry him on my back; sometimes his mother would collect him.

One day our teachers took us to see how an old windmill worked

– grinding the corn, they took us to the top of the Windmills at the Riddings, Sommercotes, and they were gutted by the fire in 1963 and finally demolished in 1963.

The teachers explained how it worked, the different size of Cog wheels that sized up to the big one that turned and ground the corn into flour.

When we got to the top there were wild pigeons nesting there, my love of pigeons got the better of me so I put one up my jumper and when we left I forgot all about the bird up my jumper till I got home and took my jumper off that I realised it was still there but it was too late to do anything then. But a good friend come down to see me and told me that a boy who used to take an apple to the teacher had told him that he saw me taking the pigeon and I let it go. But at school the next day after assembly my teacher called me out gave me four strokes of the cane on each hand and told one of the prefects to take me down to the Mill and I apologised to the man. He said okay son and back-to-school we went.

One morning we were getting ready for school and Aunt Madge was in a bad mood. We had our breakfast, bread and jam or bread and sauce she told us to go and do the washing up then get off to school. We were doing this and she come in having a good go at us. Someone must have upset her and she turned away I pulled my tongue out at her. She must have eyes in the back of her head she came back and give me a bang at the back of my head. That morning and on our way to school I said to my brother we we're going home.

We were walking along Sleetmore Lane when we met Reg Markland he was fed up as well so we started to walk back home and we had to lift off a man with a horse and cart - we could have walked faster. He gave us a few pennies and we bought a loaf and shared it between us. We walked till we got to some airfield and we stopped and was looking at the planes taking off and landing.

We started walking again and it was now getting quite dark.
We went behind the road hedges, they was slit trenches. We had been walking hours so we thought we would get some sleep.
We got into the slit trench and tried to sleep but it was cold but we were warm when we were walking so we got back onto the road. My brother Fred was saying his feet were sore. He had got Wellingtons on. We was passing this big house on the road and the people were saying goodnight to the visitors as they were leaving they said to us where was we going we said

Brummagem Bill

"to Birmingham" they said "come in and have something to eat and drink you can continue the journey later" we went in they gave something to eat and drink then they told us that they was very sorry but they had to call the police, the police come and took us down to the station.

We slept under the counter with a couple of blankets over us, the next thing was a voice saying "are these the lads" and one of our teachers said "yes they are". He and his wife had come over from Sommercotes to get us.

The police had been informed of us not coming home from school they also got in touch with our parents so there were plenty of panics all around. They took us back to the Corner house farm and made us something to eat and we went to bed. She come up to us later on in the day and said your mum and dad was to take us back home.

The teachers gave us a bit of a hard time but I was glad to be home.

After a few weeks I got some empty wooden fish boxes from the fish and chip shop on the corner of Finchley Road and Kings Road and made myself a small pen to keep some tumblers in there was quite a few flying tumblers near us I had about three pairs.   We got our tumblers from a Mr Sterkies on the corner of Burlington Street and Parliament Street, Aston.

I was up there one day for a yellow badge cock for one of my yellow hens; a chap was in the shop with a basket full of tumblers.   I asked chap if he had any yellows in there and Mr Sterkey give me a right mouthful and told me to get out of the shop and don't come back in.

 I stopped outside till the chap come out then went back in I said "I'm sorry Mr Sterkey" he said "don't you ever talk like that again while I'm making the deal now what do you want?"

I said "That yellow cock" he said "okay"

I kept my mouth shut after that.   A lesson well learned....

Chapter Three

When the 1939 War started my brother Arthur was already in the Army in the Royal Horse Artillery.   He went to Dunkirk. I was in Sidcup Road with a couple of my school mates when I looked down the road and I saw a soldier walking up, he had no hat on and as he got near I could see he was my brother.   He was grinning all over his face. I ran down to him and we walked back up to the house there was just Dad in, Mom was at the First Aid Post at the swimming baths, Warren Farm Road. They had been turned in to First Aid Posts, Dad said "go and tell your Mom

Arthurs home" and she came home with me. He was home for a while and my Mother told me some years later she had a letter from the War Office saying he was missing.

There was so many soldiers either missing or killed in action or taken prisoner at the Dunkirk. He got in touch with the Army when they got back from Dunkirk they was told they as to make their way home and wait for further instruction. He went up north to some army barracks then sent abroad again to North Africa in the 8th Army, Montgomery's lot; then worked their way into Italy, to the end of the war. He was in hospital in Rimini, Italy.

My other brother Syd went to France with the Oxford and Bucks Regiment. He met his wife there in Bayeux and married her there. Soon after the war my younger brother Fred went into the Duke of Cornwall's light infantry, on his National Service he went to Cyprus.

Back to school in the summer months me and Fred and a couple of school pals would wag it and go down to the allotment next to Perry Barr Park. There would always be plenty of fruit of all types, sometimes we would get chased off by some of the allotment owners. But this particular day we was walking up by Hawthorn Road on our way to do some scrumping and I spotted Mrs Binsley, one of our neighbours, a woman who new everybody's business. I said to my mates that's done we got to go to school. We went to school; we had plenty of time to get there. On the night our Mother came home and she said "what have you done at school today?" I knew then Old Gal Bingo had told her where she saw us. She would stand by her front gate and nose at everybody's house looking to see who went there. My mother said to us you haven't been to school. We said we had and she could go up to the school and find out. She said don't you worry I am and she did. She had a go at Bingo and she told my mother I'm only telling you what I saw. But we did have some nice neighbours; one particular woman was a Mrs Harrison. When the horse and carts used to come up, either with milk or bread or coal she would come out with a bucket and shovel to collect the horse muck. I said to her one day what do you get that for Mrs Harrison? She said "to put on my rhubarb". I said "Our Mum puts custard on ours!"

Another neighbour, she was named Mrs Sixpence, she would always be looking on the ground to see what she could find. One day she came down Sidcup Road and we were all ready. We planted a small package in the privet hedge to try this on her. We got it out and put it just under the gate with some string on it and waited. She noticed it and bent down to pick it up and we pulled it back under the gate. She just stood up and carried on walking, not turning her head around once.

There used to be an elderly man delivering the evening newspapers on his bicycle. I used to help him and he would give me a penny. I found out later on in life that he had kiosks in Birmingham City Centre at the time.

In Sidcup Road there used to be a house we called number hundreds, the woman used to sell all types of groceries, quite handy if you run out of things. I don't think she done tick though! And in Finchley Road there was a Mrs Phillips, she was my sister Elsie's piano teacher. My brothers and sister could all play the piano bar me. My brother Syd could play like Charley Coons, my uncle Albert's uncle used to come up to our house and take him to the pub on the Tyburn Road where they lived, put a cap on his head and he would play piano there. He was too young to drink at the time but made up for it in later life! People would buy him a pint and put it on top of the piano and my uncle's would drink it, they would have a whip round at the end of the night for him.

When I was fourteen I got myself a cycle, it was at the time the most popular of all bicycles, most people had one, it was called the A.S.P. "all – spare - parts" bits collected from dumps, our one was at Perry Barr. When I made my one up I went to work on it but asked my mother for my bus fare first and she said you're going on your bicycle ain't you I said yes, she said go on then or you will be late. Bus fairs used to be 6 pence workman's return then, I thought I would be better off in my pocket. My mother thought otherwise.

One Sunday morning I said to my mate Tommy Simpson I'm going to have a ride up to see my brother in law Harold. He was in the army stationed at Chilwell in Nottingham. He said I will come with you, we got to the camp site and stopped at the guard room and they phoned around but he was not on camp site so we came back home – a good ride though.

Our Mom occasionally used the Pawn Shop on the corner of Brookvale Road and Dykin Avenue, Witton. We would go over the allotment at the back of our house and come out into Clapton Grove and Ellerton Road so the neighbours would not see her. But they were all at it and when she got to the bus stop they was all there with their bundles or bags. My Mom called the Pawn Shop "Bullocks"; it was there that three balls hung outside them. I went sometimes with my sister Elsie; it was vey dark inside and a small door leading to the counter. They would charge you half pence or penny for a sheet of brown paper if yours was all ripped.

We had Daily Mail boots. Our teachers at school would check us all out to see who needed them and put our names down for some and we would go down to Digbeth Police Station in Alison Street. The teachers made sure you kept them polished, we had to stand in front of the class and they would check your hands, nails, face, ears, and your neck and if they was dirty they would send a monitor with you to the wash room and make sure you cleaned yourself up, thank God it never happened to me. I wonder what would have happened today if they brought that back into force.

At one time of my schooling we had School Dinners, it was a period when there was a general depression going on at the time. I went with my sister Elsie Saturday's and Sundays, this was only for a short period of time. My Dad used to put porridge in the oven on a night before we went to bed and it would be cooked in the morning and we would come home of a dinner time and finish it off. Mother would do rabbit stews for us, it had got to be one of the cheapest meals at the time, the rabbits was cheap and as for the vegetables, most people grew their own, my Father did.

My Mothers Father George David Whitehouse on the 16th

Brummagem Bill

December 1913 sailed from Liverpool on the Grampian Ship, Allan Line Steamship Co Ltd to St John's Newfound land with his two sons, my Uncle Joe and Bill to set up home in Canada. His occupation was a carpenter, his eldest daughter, my Aunt Elsie and her Husband had gone out earlier. He sent for my Gran and the rest of the family to join him but back in England World War One had started, 1914 and my uncle Albert had been called up in the army. My Gran said she would not come to Canada while Albert was fighting in the war so my Granddad and two uncles come back to England. In 1948 my Aunt Elsie, Mother's Sister stayed over there, her Husband with her. Later in 1948 her Husband, Uncle Fred, come over on Holiday but not my Aunt, she did not want to make the journey. It was too far for her, she would have been in her eighties at that time. My cousin Fred, he was in the Canadian Mounted Police up until he retired. He would be in his nineties now; he was still alive up until 2008.

Our cousin Joey Whitehouse from Aston was killed by the Italians on the 12th November 1942, age 23. He was in the 1st Bat. Hampshire Reg and is in Bari War Cemetery Italy. Young Joey would come over to see us at Kingstanding from time to time, our Mom made some beer once and she gave a bottle to young Joey to take home to his Dad. A few weeks later his Dad came over to see us and my Mom said "What did you think of the beer Joe?" He said "What beer?" She said "what I sent young Joey with for you to try out" He said "Wait till I get home he never give me a bottle of beer, he must have drank it on the way home". They both used to come up on their bicycles; we did not see young Joey for some time after that.

During the 1939 - 1945 war the government confiscated all the racing pigeons that members had, to get them ready trained up, and the government would take them away to various destinations including the war zones and when they arrived back at their lofts the owners would have to take the message that was done in code to the nearest police station where they would pass it onto the War office. Here it would be decoded. This sort of work was done all over the country. There was a pigeon called Winky he or she was awarded the Dicken medal for saving some airmen at sea, they were in a dingy.

My brother was brought up by his grandmother, my Dad's mum until he was 14 years of age and then he came back home. He started work at the Midland Counties Dairy's on the Kingstanding Road pushing a hand cart with milk in it and on a weekend my

Dad told me to go and help him to push the cart. His round was on roads off the Kings Road, Kingstanding. They would leave some full bottles on the side of the road for us to re-load and we would leave our empty's there and they would pick them up. Syd would swap a bottle of milk with the pop man for a bottle of pop. He packed his job in and went in to the Greengrocery trade until he was called up for National Service in the army, Oxford and Bucks Light Infantry.

Chapter Four

I left school at 14 years and started as a plumber's mate at a place called E.J. Sands Ltd on the corner of Crompton Road and Heathfield Road, Handsworth.

There were three of us starting, we had to wait in the workshop till the plumbers come in. One of the plumbers was a Mr Jim Tranter he would be about the same age as my dad, he said come with me "son" he said "what's your name" I said "Bill" he said "pick up that big bag of tools Bill, let's go".

Our first job was at Anthony Road School, Alum Rock. The school had been bombed and we had to repair burst pipes and seal some off. On the way to Anthony Road school we got on a tram Mr Tranter told me to call him Jim. It seems so strange calling a man my father's age by his first name he said "do you want a cigarette Bill?" I took it. "Thank you" I said. It was first one I ever had. The tram was rocking from side to side and I felt very sick, I put my hand with my cigarette down the side of me and dropped it on the floor. He never offered me another one and thank God I never took it up. I was so glad to get a cup of tea to take the taste away.

We got to Anthony Road school and the caretaker showed us where the trouble was then Jim said "go and get some water in this tea can" I got the water and he put a chisel in the wall near the ground, hung the tea can onto it started the blow Lamp up and put the tea can on it. Within 10 minutes we had a nice cup of tea and washed the bad taste of the fag away.

EJ Sands Ltd had got the contract for all the schools in Birmingham and at the time so we covered the lot. One day we had to go to Erdington cottage homes in Reservoir Rd, Erdington. It was a private road with big houses on either side with large playing fields they was for the children with problems at home. We come to this one home to do a burst pipe and in the playing area two little girls came up to me and said "hello Bill" I could not believe it there was my two cousins of my dad's sister.   I went home on the night and told my Mom and Dad but we already had one of their sisters, Shirley, my Mum and Dad adopted her when she was young, my two cousins was only in there for a short time.

We were working at a school in Moseley Road and there were some men doing a flat roof brushing hot tar onto it.   I was walking past and some come down onto my head, I was rushed into the kitchen and the cook got some margarine and a pair of scissors she cut what was really matted together and massaged the margarine into the rest of my head after she had done that I washed my hair, what I got left, and went home.

Another incident, we was working on some cottage at Kinlet, the other side of Kidderminster, they was new cottages and had scaffolding poles put in wooden barrels with the chains wrapped round the poles and a nail to keep them together. They were starting to take it down when my mate asked the Foreman if they could leave it up till we had put the guttering all around. It was agreed to and we started to work. I was walking along the scaffold when I stepped on to one of the planks, I went down and the plank followed me. I landed up on a pile of broken house bricks. The plank was not resting on a batten and you could not see it from above, the others were covering it up. My mate rushed over and we went to our truck I sat down a while and the foreman come over to see if I was all right I said I was and he said "Bill go straight back up and carry on, if you don't you might not want to climb again" with that he bandaged my hand up and I carried on working.

We were working in a posh house in Westminster Road Handsworth putting some new copper pipes and a new back boiler in. Mr Sands said to me bring your house slippers tomorrow I said "I don't have any slippers sir", he said "you will have to work in your socks then" and that's what I did. My mate said "you might have put on a pair with no holes in" I said "all my socks have holes in." Mr Sands come to see us, took one look at my socks gave me a dirty look and went. We were only there for two days and we were back to normal.

Brummagem Bill

When I was fifteen years of age I joined the Aston Amateur Boxing Club at the Holt Public House Aston. Our Manager was a Mr Albert Hodder. It was a well known club, one of my mates Tommy Simpson came along with me. There were several clubs around the Birmingham area and we would go and have competitions with them. One tournament, one of our boxers, a lad named Jones half way through a round, his father got in the ring and was having a go at the Ref'. We all thought it might lead up to an unscheduled fight but it did not. They had some useful boxers, there were two brothers, the Bennets, Tommy Lawley, and there were quite a few names I forget. A lot went away to war we would go across the road into Aston Park and do some training if the weather was right. On Sunday morning me and me mate would go to Perry Barr Park, we'd get there nice and early and have the rowing boats out. If it was quiet the park keeper wouldn't bother to call you in, this was the best, to be early. It would be dinner time when we got home; we would have dinner, wash up afterwards then go down to the park in Finchley Road to our mates.

My brother Fred was very particular with his clothes and how he dressed.
He wore kid gloves and if he had a hole in his socks he would turn the sock so the hole would be in front behind the tongue and

lacing. Clothes was rationed the same as food during the war, you had clothing coupons. This was I think when the three-piece suit went out of fashion. You had to give more coupons for a three piece suit than you did for a two piece, so you used the extra coupons for a shirt.

At 14 when I started Dancing we would go to a place called "Madam Aimee's School of Dancing" on the Chain Walk, off Lozells Road. There were footprints painted on the floor to show you various moves and how to place your feet. She would dance with you and her Husband would dance with the girls to music from records.

We also went to our old school, Peckham Road, for dancing on Saturday night; most of all our school pals went. We all had two left feet to start with but we got the hang of it as the saying goes. A lot of us met our future wives - I did at 16, we got married on August 10, 1946, we will be celebrating our diamond wedding in August 2006.

Our school band consisted of two violinist's, father and son (the son, we all thought suffered from sleeping sickness, he used to drop off to sleep when playing) and another son on drums and a pianist Arthur Pulley, he was a cripple he also played the accordion. He joined ENSA an organisation who entertain the troops home and abroad when he come home on leave he would come and entertain us at the school dance hall. We used to go on Sunday night to Maryvale Old Oscott Hill. We would dance to records of Victor Sylvester on an old windup gramophone and on Tuesday we would have our band from Saturday, the war was on but it did not stop us from enjoying ourselves.

At 16 I joined the police cadets at Kingstanding with my mates Harold Crook - that's a good name for a police cadet! - Frank Williams - not related.

We would go out in pairs on very minor incidents or take messages to police officers. The police stations was all covered with sand bags so was swimming baths at Warren farm road that had been turned into a first-aid post, my mother was there as the Red Cross nurse.

Back at work we had a job at a dentist in Lozells Road, Handsworth, the following day I went to work but got as far as Lozells Road, Six Ways Aston and it was closed and a police officer told me "You won't be working here today there are still unexploded mines in James Road". So we went back to the yard, told the Gaffer and he gave us some tools and we had tools from some of the other plumber till we was able to go back to Lozells Road. It was the same time that the Lozells Cinema had been hit and the Manager lost his life.

We would go to quite a few places to do bomb damage repairs; some would be still smouldering from the night or day before. Mount Pleasant Rookery Handsworth was another place we worked on. We were at another Dentist at the Soho Road near the turning of the Rockery Road.   My mate sent me back to the yard for some fittings, it was lunchtime so I had it at the yard, Mr Sands son's car was parked outside - a Rover - I was having a look at the inside and I noticed he had left the ignition key in.

I thought I wonder if I could just move it a bit without being seen, I started the engine up and the old kangaroo went straight into action.   I finished half way across the Heathfield Road.

The 29 bus come down and started tooting his horn and Mr Sands looked out of the office windows, spotted his son's car in the middle of the road. He came out spluttering on his cigarette, his words were "get out get out! I have a good mind to fetch the police" he got in the car and reversed it back into its place.

I went back into the yard and said I was sorry "can have these fittings for the job in Soho Road" he said "you stay there, the police want to talk to you, are in serious trouble" the police man came and he said what "was your intentions?"

I said "I just wanted to see if I could move it a bit, just out of curiosity"

He wrote out a statement and said he would be seeing me again. In the meantime Mr Sands had taken the fittings up to my mate, by the time he finished writing out the statements it was time for me to get home.

When I arrived home there was only my sister in, I said where's Mum she said she has gone out. Half-hour later she come in and I said "where have you been?" "I'll tell you where I have been, I've been to Lozells police station" and with that she gave me a right hiding going over, "I'm not telling your dad, you can tell him."

I did not tell him.

That night I had enough off my mother, the next day at work we was working away and the dentist come in and said "the police wants to speak to Mr William Wintle" my stomach turned over. I thought "this is it". Ten years in the nick, or five for good behaviour. I went to the phone it was a chief inspector he said "Billy, will you be at home about eight o'clock tonight?" I said yes "Will your father be home as well?" I said yes. He said I will see you there. My dad was in the kitchen having his tea and he said what you standing there for "I'm in trouble Dad" (I was scared stiff) he said "what bloody trouble?"

I just managed to get it out when the door knocked it was the inspector and a sergeant who said to my dad "you know why we are here Mr Wintle?" he said "yes, he has just told me", they read the riot act at me in a very nice way - driving without out a license and under-age without insurance, driving dangerously on the Kings Highway, taking the car without the owners consent. My father said "what's going to happen to him then?" He said Mr Sands had decided not to go through with a charge, the inspector said you are very very lucky but if I get into any similar trouble they will bring this case back into it.

My mother and father come up to my works with me the following morning. I apologised to Mr Sands with my parents then thanked him for not pressing the charge.

A couple of weeks later Mr Sands said "Billy would you like to have a week end with me and my wife at our bungalow by the river" I think it was near Stourport "but ask your parents first" they both said yes and the following weekend we went. They had a nice rowing boat; it was a wooden bungalow they took me to a riverside pub for our lunch, a really nice weekend.

I realise now that if they had charged me for my driving offences their son Stanley would have to be charged as well leaving the car keys in the ignition It was a criminal offence and more so during the war.

Chapter Five

I was coming up to 17 now and wanted a change of place. I was told they was looking for a plumber's mate to work at the swimming baths so I went up to Kent baths Department and I got the job there, was provided with two pairs of overalls, we had them cleaned at Woodcock Street baths.

They used to do all the laundry for the washing baths. People went there if they had no means of bathing at home. Anyway, I got the job there as their plumber was off sick with a hernia; they gave me several jobs to go to. One was at Harbourn. I had done one or two jobs here. One man in charge told me to take my time; I was doing them too fast, that it would look bad on Sam when he came back to work. I said that I had not been used to this at E.J. Sands - they had a good idea how long a job would take and that's what I was working on. He said Sam would have taken a couple of days; I thought I would be too bored working like that. After that I took my time it was dead boring. Sam came back a couple of weeks later, he was a small chap with bowler hat and waxed moustache, tight jacket sleeves, a bit on the short side. He was a cheese and onion and a pint of ale man at the nearest pub, he would come back hold his arms up as though he was dancing with someone, went whistling to the tune of the Blue Danube. You could not help but laugh at him. He said to me "one day Bill I have to go into town to pay my rates", he said he won't be long I didn't see him till the next day.

The war was over now and all the swimming baths that had been converted into first aid posts had to be changed back. There was a lot of work dismantling, where the main swimming pools was they had been turned into different sized rooms for different purposes. Some was zinc lined, all the windows was blacked out with very thick black paint. We had to use a very strong jelly type of paint remover containing caustic soda.

I was coming up to my 18th birthday so I volunteered for the RAF at Birmingham; they sent me to RAF Padgate Warrington. I told them at Birmingham I wanted to be trained as a driver mechanic, that's what they put me down for when. I got to RAF Padgate the NCO they said "sorry there's no more vacancies for that trade" they said there is for firemen and cooks. I said I don't want either, I was going in for 21 years service I wanted a choice. They said I don't blame you! Sorry. So I went back to Birmingham.

The next morning I went back up to the recruitment centre and told them what they said, they had a good laugh and said we will give you a letter and send you back up the next day. They put me down for M.T.R.I motor transport repair inspection. And then we were sworn in they said that this is your last chance to say what you want to do your 21 years or 14 years or just the duration of present emergency. I took the latter. They kitted me out and sent me with about 10 others to RAF Yatesbury Wiltshire we were met with a truck and taken to our billets then marched to pick up our bedding - three blankets and a pillow the following morning reveille 06.00hrs breakfast at 07.00hrs Parade 08.00hrs

We had eight weeks basic training to do before we was posted to different camps we completed our basic training in seven weeks I got a first saving certificate best recruit - 15 shillings was good money in 1946 and was recommended for the drill instructors course.

I was posted to RAF Base Snitterfield near Stratford-upon-Avon I got home every week end with my two Brummie pals, we would thumb a lift from the bottom of the lane at Bearley Cross.   A hearse came a long one day I thumbed it down and got in, he said I stopped for two of your mates they took one look at me and told me to carry on. He said that they will have to have a ride in one some day! He laughed, took me as far as Robin Hood Lane, I got the bus the rest of the way home.

We had prisoners of war here Germans and Italians some worked at the RAF base and others worked in local farms, some of them never went back and married local girls. We was living in Nisson huts we had several of our own prisoners of war returning from Japan and Germany, one chap in our hut was about 6 foot tall, my mate said "Bill Pick this chap up" and I did, it was like picking a two-year-old, his eyes were at the back of his head and had that vacant smile on his face, another six months in captivity and I think he would be in some far away cemetery.   I think all the returning prisoners from war camps should have gone to convalescent homes.   I was thumbing a lift one night and a chap come down on his motorcycle and stopped and asked where I was I going, I said Birmingham he said what part I said Kingstanding, he said I can give you a lift to Short Heath, I said that would be great.   I got the 28 bus to Hawthorn Road and then the 33 bus. I will get the bus to town next morning then the Shirley bus to

Monkspath and get a lift from there. Sometime this chap on his motorcycle would come and it would stop and give me a lift back to the camp. After a few lifts off this chap I asked him where he worked he said in the offices, he turned out to be one of my officers he was picking me up taking me I had no sleeping out pass, if they picked me up in the morning, would always drop me off at the guard room I would pop in look at the clock and go to the billet and get myself ready for parade.

This camp was nice and handy for me I didn't bother to go to the drill instructors course I stayed put – I was home most weekends one weekend I went home we started talking about getting married I mentioned it to my mother and she said you are too young wait till you come out of the RAF but I kept on about it. You had to have your parents consent if you was under 21. But something conveniently happened; Doris became pregnant. I went into Birmingham and got the forms for her to sign; she went quiet; I left and went up to Doris's house I stayed late and when I got home my mother was still waiting for my father to come down the stairs, they asked me why the rush to marriage I said I loved Doris and I want to marry her. She said there's nothing wrong with her is there I said yes she is carrying my baby. Dead silence surrounded the room before the explosion my dad was the first to start he said – you have brought shame on your family, they will not want to know you.

I went to bed and the next morning I come downstairs, I looked at the forms, no signatures, as went on to Doris's mum and dad's there was no problem with them.

When I got back home on the night the forms had been signed they said that they would not be coming to the wedding my brother Fred came, he was my best man, we arranged it for the 10th of August 1946.   It was a Saturday and it teamed down with rain, we went to town on the bus that had a gas tank on the back to save petrol, we got into town the rain never stopped we all got soaked.   We all had carnations that was grown in Doris mother's back garden, we took some extra in case someone else turned up and they did it was my mother.   She started performing; Doris's mother said if she carried on like this she would get the police. When we got inside to the registrar he performed the marriage and he asked for witnesses to come forward my mother said is it right for the young people to put their signatures the registrar said yes as long as parents have signed the forms he said its okay. Well I will sign and Doris's mum signed, the registrar said congratulations and good luck it's been a bad start but it will get better.   I wonder if he was referring to the weather or my mother's attitude.

I must say at this stage as the years went by my mother's attitude towards Doris changed and she told Doris she wished she had been like her with her family, she said she will never be lonely you are a wonderful mother. We went back to Doris's mother's house we had corned beef sandwiches with lemonade and a good night was had by all. We went to bed. I had been used to sleeping on my own so it was very warm and I couldn't sleep. We come downstairs the mother in law was up and we stayed up eating toast and drinking tea for a couple of hours.

Chapter Six

When I first started to go up to Doris' mothers house all the children was still at school, except Florrie, she was in the Land Army and Frank, who I think was working at a garage down by the Broadway Perry Bar. Anne was in her last year at school, the twins Peggy and Patty were in the senior girls, Mary and Johnny was still in the juniors.

My first night up there Frank was messing about with an old wireless, the Mother in Law had this old wireless for years. It ran on accumulators. She would have one on charge down at the ironmongers on the Kings Road; we would take it down each week. Mrs Williams, as I called her at the time (but later 'Mom' because she was another Mom to me) liked a small bet on the Pools and the "Gee Gee's". One week, she won over one hundred pounds – a lot on money in those days. One of the first things she bought was an all electric radio. On the first night she got Radio Athlone, an Irish station, who used to give you some tips on horses that were running the next day. He would give you his best three I remember them still to this day, they was 'Flower Dust', 'Reminiscent' and (I'm not sure how this was spelt) 'Rhar the Second'. And they all come up! I don't bet but that day I did. Mom had the cheque from returned from the Pools in nice frame for her to display.

One night I come home and the Evening Mail had been put through the door. I took it upstairs, wrote three of the winners down in doubles as she had shown me a few days ago, come back downstairs and folded the paper up and put it by the door. Then I went up the garden and had my pigeons out. After an hour I went in the house, I took the slip of paper out and asked Mom to check it. She said "well you have a winner", then she said "You have a double", then she said "you have a treble up". She worked everything out for me; I would have had a nice bit to come. She said we don't need Radio Athlone if you can pick them as good as that! My guilt hit me – how am I going to turn this around? Doris knew what I had done. Then Dad came in, she said Bill's had a Treble today! He looked at me; my left eye was batting fifty to the dozen. He could see I was having a joke with Mom.

I told him after what I had done, she just laughed it off. Mom's bet would be 3.4d cross doubles and a 4d treble. I wonder if a bookmaker would take a bet like that today?!

Chapter Seven

Doris's mum was a very special person to me and all who knew her and her husband Frank he was in the Second World War. He served in North Africa and Italy. She had eight children at home during the first part of the war and she had to feed and clothe them. A real tough job! She had what we used to call a "gammy" arm she had a major operation many years ago. When Doris's Mom Dolly would wash the sheets we would help her to fold them after she had hand wringed them through the wringer. Then out on the line to dry. When they were dry they would be folded again and put through the wringer to press them.

She done all her washing with the maid and tub she had a cast-iron wringer outside which she would swing the wringer round like nothing at all, she had the well-known boiler stick that I have felt the end of many times.

I would give the world to feel it again from her she was a lovely woman and Doris is a replica of her mother in looks and ways but she hasn't cracked me on the back of the head with the boiler stick. I think she would have if we had one.

Saved by the washing machine!
After a cooling off period of my parents they got in touch with us and we was invited down to the house for tea. We went up quite often. After a time my mother said the big room is empty would you like to come and stay I said we will think about it, it was a bit crowded down at Doris's mother's house and it seemed a good idea at the time. So the next time we went up she mentioned it again and we said we would take it and Valerie was born here in my mother and father's bed, they was in France at the time at my brother and his wife's place.

In December 1946 I was granted three months compassionate leave from the RAF, any service men under 21 did not get marriage allowance, my case was one of the first to go to Parliament so I come home and went to work till our baby was born a girl Valerie Patricia on the 23 March 1947, soon after I had to go back. I was posted to RAF Pershore Worcester, it was a nice camp they had a nice gymnasium. I joined the boxing club we went for cross-country running early mornings we had late breakfasts plus extra food after a few months my mother started her unpleasant ways again and it was Doris who was getting it when I was away. I had some leave coming up so we decided to go over to see her sister Florrie in Shipston on Stour. We had a couple of days and she asked Doris if we would like to go and stay there Doris told me, I said yes it would do you good so we went my mother who tried to persuade us against it but we went. It was a very old cottage in new street. I used to cycle from Pershore on the weekends; we both like the country so we were happy.

Before my demob there was courses for RAF personnel to go out on, I put myself on an agriculture course at RAF Bassington near Royston Cambridge. I finished that and came back to RAF Pershore until I was demobbed then I went on a civilian

Brummagem Bill

agricultural course.

I was placed in Shipston and worked through Mr Seymour at Weston Mill Cherrington Hill, a gentleman farmer he had a married son who also worked for him. He would call to see you and move you if you need be. I was working most of the time with a man called Ernest Randall - nice chap, his hobby was buying young horses and breaking them in.
He had a field over at Cherrington; he taught me how to harness up a horse and cart. He lived At Tiddmington opposite where the young Mr Seymour lived. That had land scattered around Shipston, at Honnington he had some highland cattle, one had got husk. We had to give him some doses of medicine out of a pint bottle every time Stow fair was on and Ernie Randall said "Bill be off to Stow tomorrow with two horses, you can ride the grey cob and I will take the bay mare" it was held in the main road then in 1948.

The one he was selling was a big bay mare he told me to get on her and just trot her up and down the road he said I shall be by the mobile tea van when you see me put my hand up go to the railings and tie her up. I done this and went over to him we had a cup of tea he said there was a couple looking at you and they have just gone over to her, he said stay there I will come back to you.   He was over there for about three quarters of an hour and he come over and said she's sold.

They was selling little welsh pony's I said to Ern if my daughter was older I would get one for her "would you?" he said I said yes he said which one would you pick I said that black beauty he said "go on I will lend you the money" so I got Valerie her pony.   He picked two and we both got on the grey mare and the three ponies followed us back to Ern's field but the black pony become a bit too much for a child pony so I asked Ern if he would swap for the little quiet one and he said "yes" .

Chapter Eight

We felt settled at Florries and Bernard's.   Doris had got a job around the corner a small factory to do with fishing reels.   We come downstairs one morning and there was a note on the shelf from Florrie asking us to find somewhere else to live so Doris and

Brummagem Bill

Valerie went back to stay at her mothers house. I stayed at Shipston, we was at Honnington hay making. I took a case with me with some food in on the night and I put the ladder up to the haystack climbed up and pulled the ladder up, I done this for two weeks one day one of the workers saw me coming down "Bill, what you doing up there?" I said that's where my bed is at the moment, we had to get out of Doris's sisters house, she left a note on the shelf for us told us she wanted our rooms so that's why I am sleeping up here. Doris and the baby have gone back to Birmingham to her mother's house. He spoke to Mr Seymore and he said he would have a ride down to the police station and to see if he could get me somewhere to stay.

In the meantime Ernie Randall had a word with his sister who lived in New street Shipston and she said I could stay there till such a time when I find somewhere so I stayed there a couple of weeks, Ernie Randall moved our furniture from Florrie's on that Sunday morning with a tractor and a trailer. We got everything out except the wardrobe that was it. Mr Seymour Jr. said I could put it in his wood shed; it was there for several weeks. I was going home at weekends. Ernie Randall bought an ex ministry mobile office from a place in Claverdon. He put it in his field, we put a couple of beds in and we moved in there.

Brummagem Bill

I would have the Stratford Journal every week to look for any work with cottages, but it was just after the war and housing was very short and as quick as they became empty they was filled up again. I had one reply from Ragley Hall Alcester. I went for my interview and they said we will let you know.

Two days later Mr Seymore come and said "Bill I've got two places for you to look at. Make arrangements for your wife to come over and I will take you round to them". The first one was a waste of time. The second one was at Barford near Warwick. He wanted someone very quick. He took us all round the farm then took us to see the cottage; it was in Church Road Barford. The toilet was up the garden two wooden holes with a tin container underneath. The men would come during the night and empty them. There was two pig stys at the top of the garden it was a two bedroom a front room and a kitchen living room with an old type sink with a hand pump for your water supply. We could move in straight away. He had a herd of cows, pigs and chickens. I told him I had no knowledge of cows but some of pigs and chickens, he said that's ok and wanted us to start straight away, so we accepted and moved in. The following week I had a letter for my final interview at Ragley hall Alcester – I had to cancel it. We moved into Church road Barford and

Brummagem Bill

started to work for Mr Sparks.

It was a 5.30 start, it was machine milking, and the first thing I had to do was to start the milking machine up. Then get the cows from out of the field into the sheds, feed them and milk them. Put the milk through the cooling system and into the churns. Mark them up and take them to the top of the drive and put on the platform for the milk board to collect. Then go for your breakfast with your pint of milk. After that come back and clean and sterilize all the units and pipes, clean the sheds, stock sheds, feed the chickens. At 3.30 start all over again. On a Tuesday night you would have to stay a bit late.

Weighing the milk from each cow, and they was fed according to how much milk they was producing. When harvesting was on it was late nights until it had finished Christmas came the farmer gave me a cockerel and half dozen eggs for Valerie. In the New Year my birthday was on the seventh of January I was 21.   I went to work as normal at the end of the day he told me that he wanted someone with more experience who he could leave days and go on his holidays.   Happy birthday Bill wages was for £4.10 1 pint milk a day rent free cottage. At this point I thought of going back in the RAF I told our next neighbour what had happened and she said is he from London I said yes she said he come up some time ago but he could not start until the New Year he had looked over the house I did meet him later. So the so called farmer just wanted me to cover till he was available.

So Doris, Valerie and I went back to Birmingham. Doris and Valerie went to Doris's mother's house, there was no room for me here at the time so I went on stayed with my oldest brother and his wife Arthur and Joan.

I brought the pony back from the Shipston on Stour and I rented a field on the corner of Chester Road and Baker Lane for 10 shillings a week. My Dad told me there was an air raid shelter at HP Sauce if I wanted it for nothing. I hired a hand cart from off the College Road, Erdington and pushed it to HP Sauce Aston Cross, loaded it on and pushed it back to the field in Sutton Coldfield. Later the lady I rented it off told me I could not put it up as she would have to pay rates on the land. What a wasted journey and time – a good twelve mile walk!

I got a job on the railways at the old new Street station as a porter sorting parcels at the cage - on number 10 platform, you would put them on different barrows there was about 20 barrows and when they was full a tractor driver would come and take them to different platforms after six months a vacancy came up for a tractor driver I put my name down and went on a course at

Brummagem Bill

Sutton Coldfield station and come back as a tractor driver.

I got myself a motorcycle a BSA 350.   It was handy for the 6 till 2 shift.   Sunday mornings was a bad service.   I was going to work one morning and having some trouble with the electrics, so I took it into Lucas's Great Kings street, they said leave it with us to sort out. The following day I phoned them they said it is not ready yet there was trouble with the electrics they would have to rewire it A couple of days went by and they said it was ready I went down to the office and they presented me with a large bill; I took one look at it and said "it's a lot of money for re wiring my motorcycle" he said "have you seen it?" I said "no" he said "come and have a look at it". He took me over and said "we have made a good job of it". They had put a new headlamp on a new magneto, new rear lamps, new rewiring I said "look I have no money for that lot" he said "you have got almost a new bike".   I said "I didn't tell you to put all these things on, put my old ones back on and I will pay for the re-wiring".   He said "we can't do that they were put on the scrapheap".   I said "I can't pay" he said "sell the bike then" and walked back to his office.
I went home and told my brother about it he said "come on lets go down the road to have a word with my father-in-law" who was in the police force. We told him all about it and he said "they haven't got a dogs chance to get all that money, they

have made a mistake and they have got to pay for it". So I went down the next day with my brother. The manager says "can you pay this much then" I said "no". He said "you have almost a new bike out there", he said "how much can you pay then?" I said "this is all I have", "give it here" he said "I would have the next bloke who comes in here with a Rolls-Royce".

After a time Doris's sister moved out of her mother's house so I was able to go and live a normal married life again.

We used to get free travel passes we went to Weston for a day out that was the only train pass I ever had.

Brummagem Bill

Plates

Brummagem Bill

Windmills at Riddings, Ripley
And Corn Mills

Riddings corn mills were built in 1877 by James Oakes and named after James and his wife, Sarah. The mills ceased working in 1927. In 196. they were gutted by fire, listed as unsafe and wer subsequently demolished.

Brummagem Bill

Emily Harriet Whitehouse
My Mother's Mother and her neighbours
Daughter

My Father and Mother:

Arthur J C Wintle
Emily Harriet Wintle

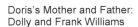

Doris's Mother and Father:
Dolly and Frank Williams

Brummagem Bill

Evacuation
From left to right: Brother Fred, Me,
Harold Cornfield and the Aunts Nephew

Coronation Day, me
with a neighbour
Bill Wintle, Agnes
Hope and my Dad with
his hands in his
pockets.

He would have told us
off
if we did it!

Corner House Farm Derby

Birchwood
Methodist School

This was the
school that we
went to. The near
windows was that
of our classroom

Brummagem Bill

Me, somewhere in Germany

The Championship Cup "Thurso"

Great Uncle Sid Haines

Police Cadets, Age 16

Brummagem Bill

Billy, Maryann, David, Linda, John
Pauline, Me, Doris, Valerie

Haines Gloucester & Cheltenham carriers and general
haulier. Gt granddad, James Arthur Sid Haines; Father
& 2 Sons

Brummagem Bill

Me and Doris at Orchard Cottage

After The hunt!!

Brummagem Bill

Ch. Tantaus Royal Lass. Bred by me and
sold to Mr & Mrs B Hadland of Stockton
Wire's, Yardley, Birmingham

Me feeding the Bull I bred Bildor Blazaway. I sold it to
Mr & Mrs Limb
at Solers Farm, Solers Hope in Hereford.

The type of cart I would help our Syd push of a
weekend

The Big White House, Cockermouth.

Brummagem Bill

Me, Pauline & Keith in Prague

<u>Chapter Nine</u>

Doris's mother had a nice garden quite large; I kept a few tumbler pigeons at the top end. I left the railway and got a job at the swimming baths in Warren farm road. Soon after this Doris became pregnant with our son Billy. He was born at Marston Green Maternity hospital in October it was shortly after that we were offered a place of our own it was a Hawksley bungalow at number 9 Lea Croft Avenue Lea village. It was a brand new three-bedroom house. It was near Chelmsley Wood; a green belt area at that particular time, nice countryside. Our second daughter Linda was born there too.

At the time I had started working with my father-in-law and brother-in-law on nights at then McNamara's haulage firm; now BRS. I soon got a job near our home at Richards, Marston Green they made prams and invalid chairs. I was on the riveting bench and after a while the plumber got the sack. I was quite friendly with the electrician and he said that they was in a bit of a mess, the plumber had got the job half finished in the drying rooms. I told him I'd done some plumbing and I could finish the job, he told the boss and he had me in the office. I told him what I needed and he said do this job and you can have the job permanently, so that's what happened. I was there till the place closed down.

There was no redundancy money or paid holidays so when my holidays come round I got casual jobs with my father in law who was now working at Smiths Brewery Lichfield Road Aston, he got me a job there for my two weeks holiday.

Now I had to get a job quick, a chap also from Richards prams went to the Morris motors Drews Lane, the personnel officers asked us what we wanted. I said is there any vacancy for capstan and milling machines operators? He said yes, he gave me a card - he called it an introduction card - take it to Washwood Heath employment exchange and then come back here. When I got back he said when can you start? I said now he said, No Monday morning will do fine.

Monday morning came and so did the butterflies, I had not worked on any types of machinery. I was taken to the tractor shop introduced to the foreman and he took me to the charge hand. He took me over to the machine I was to operate, it was a big capstan - you pushed a two inch diameter long bar through till it was sticking through the jaws and tied them up with a chuck key. He gave me a good demonstration and left it to me; he had only gone about half an hour when there was such a bang. I ducked there were shouts and everyone started laughing and shouting. The setter came over to look at the machine and said where was the chuck key I had tightened it up without taking the chuck key out.   He took me off that that machine and put me on one which was much smaller, he said what type of machines had I worked on and I come clean and told him I had just been made redundant and I needed some work so he put me on simple jobs and gradually worked me up onto the big jobs showing me how to sharpen tools and drills. He told me one day that our shop was closing down and was moving to Wales, he said there was a vacancy in another shop on the Automatics and told me to go and see a Dick Moulton which I did and he said I could start whenever I could.

I started the following Monday and I had a week on days and started regular nights the following week.

I stayed here till we moved house to Northfield at no 50 Crossland Rd, this was a nice area.   I got a transfer to the Austin motors the East Works Longbridge, working nights on steering arms.

I got myself a loft and a few racing pigeons and flew the South Road. Our secretary was Jack Maily who also worked at the Austin in Longbridge. I went to work one night and we all picked our wages up and they gave us our P45's, all the nightshift was laid off and you got no redundancy pay in those days. We all thought there was going to be a general slump so I went to the new street railway station to see if there were any vacancies and they said there was a vacancy for a truck shunter and porter at Cotteridge, Kings Norton. I worked at Cotteridge on the platform and when we need to put freight trucks on the train. We used to use a long pole with a hook on the end lift the links up and hook them up and un hook them they all had to be in the right order I was only here for a short time.

An old pal of mine Tommy Simpson, his wife's brother another Tommy, lived at the bottom of our road and we bumped into each other. I was going to work on nights we got chatting and he said "work with us"
I said what do you do? he said on the knocker I said I can't do that I thought he meant knocking stuff off he explained to me he was working for a London firm selling carpets and blankets from door-to-door and credit or cash sales then the firm would sell the debt to well known large firms. He said he earned more then me in a day that I got in a week! I said I would try my luck I was on nights the next weeks so I went in on the Monday morning, he took me to a couple of doors and he said all you have to do and I said okay.

Brummagem Bill

The first I went to the woman must have felt sorry for me she bought two off me and went in a few more doors before I sold another carpet.   I think I sold seven that day, 8 shillings a carpet and a basic week of three pounds the next week I met my supervisor there was four salesmen, two on either side of the road.

When we have signed someone up we always seem to get a cup of tea, if not we would ask for a cup of water, and that would do the trick, a bit cheeky really.

We were always dry selling! All the talking made us thirsty.

Chapter Ten

After a year I was made supervisor. I had a Ford Transit van and four salesmen based at Walsall. We had certain areas to build up along the way. We had what we called R.D.S Rank – don't serve bad payers. They come from all walks of life. Some big posh houses were as bad as the rough looking houses. If you happen to serve a R.D.S you had to get the goods back out of the house. If you could not you would have to pay for it yourself and sometimes that did happen.

I was walking in the Winson Green area of Birmingham and sold carpets and blankets to this woman and her mother was visiting her. I sold to her and when I took the orders in to the office they threw them out. I had to go and get them back. I got the daughters back and I had to go to Aston to her mother's house. It was night time and her husband was having his tea. He was not happy, she called me in and after going through the purse full of pawn tickets I got the one for the blankets. The next morning I went to the pawn shop and paid out of my own pocket for the two pairs of blankets. The pawn broker said, "we always know when your salesmen have been round as we get full up with carpets, blankets, sheets, kettles, you name it! You see they paid 2/6 old money deposit for a carpet or any item and they would pawn it for a few quid. Sometimes we had no trouble in getting them out and sometimes you had no chance.

Every Thursday you had a stock check in your van by your area manager and if your stock was down through this you would borrow off another Supervisor.

This sort of thing went on week after week. This job was a liability.

You had to stamp your own cards, pay for your petrol and you had a very small basic wage. You had to pay for any losses and you got a very small commission off your salesman orders. You had the use of a van for your own personal use - that was the only good thing about it.

There was quite a few firms starting up and more teams operating in Birmingham. We always seem to be following them around at the finish. The public got fed up with sales people knocking on their doors. They would come to the windows and shake their heads - very disheartening at times.

But we used to turn some of these into fun...like the woman who was in her front garden trying to measure it up for turf, she asked for advice. We took the belt off our macs and measured the space 9 belts by 12 belts, plus the buckle. She wrote it down and put the order in. The next time we were around, we checked it out and all was well. We used to call at a cafe in Blake Lane off the Bordesley Green Road, there was a chap used to work at a small factory. He came up for sandwiches for the workers. He said he was fed up with his job so we offered him a job cleaning cars one hundred pounds a week. He said he would start next week, we said "what about now". We said we would give him a lift down to his works, he jumped into the car and we took off. We crossed over the main Bordesley Green Road, down Churchill Road and he said, "You've gone past my works". We put our finger in his back and told him we was going to hold up a bank and if he wanted a hundred pounds a week wage he would have to help out.

We turned into Colonial Road and he started kicking his legs all over the place.
We let him go. There was some Giro men in the road doing some repairs work, he ran up to them and we rode off. The next morning we went in to the same cafe, told the woman owner what we had done. We had a good laugh, she told us off and we waited for him to come in for the sandwiches. When he arrived we poked our faces around the corner and said, "How are you today", he said he had told his boss and he had informed the

Police. We said, "So, you didn't want the job then", he said, "No, I'm staying where I am". (I honestly regret all this now.)

There was another time when we were working in Erdington. I was talking to a chap who was a gardener, I said, "I don't like gardening, as a matter of fact I hate it!" He said, "Have you got much?" I said, "No, about 20 yards by 8 yards". He asked me where I lived; I gave him my Dads address, 28 Sidcup Road, Kingstanding. He said he could help me out if I liked, I said I had a chap looking after it for me but he was not much good. He said, "How much do you pay?" £3.00 or 30 shillings per hour. He said, "I will do it for you for £1.00 per hour. I said, "O.K., you can start this weekend" I said "you will have to take your own tools", he said "no problem", I said,

"Go up the back entry; if the other bloke is there just tell him that you are taking over his job". He arrived on Saturday morning, my Dad was up the garden as usual and this chap went up to my Dad and told him that he is the new gardener and "you have been sacked" and that he was taking over. My Dad told him where to go in no uncertain terms. He told my Mother he would kill me when he saw me.

Chapter Eleven

This canvassing job with carpets and bedding bales was getting to be very hard work. Too many other companies were doing the same thing. There was a new firm starting in Birmingham selling sixpence 'in the slot' televisions so I applied for selling the sixpence slot televisions and started work the next week. I had a Wolseley 680 Saloon car, you would sell a TV and go back the next week and take the rental money out of the box and what was left in the box you would try and sell them furniture on the hire purchase. Some just took the surplus cash.

We had Balsall Heath areas, I did the one part of the estate, and my mate Tom did the other side. It was canvasser's paradise but it had its down falls. I went several times to some houses and they would be out and some had moved out, took the TV with them, and did not inform the company. One of my customers was pushing a pram up the road with our TV in it. I went over and she said I was going to let you know. I had been looking for this customer for weeks, I was glad to get it back. Another customer had put a candle on top of the TV, let it burn through the top of the TV. I could not get an answer from this customer's house so I went back on the Sunday dinnertime. She was not happy, neither was I! It was this time that I discovered the damage that had been done so I took the TV out of the house with a few swear words ringing in my ears. The thing that went through my mind was "I hope you burnt your Sunday joint". I think the firm would have got some insurance back off this.

I packed the job in and went and got another job driving for Ansell's Brewery. My Mother was a Nurse there and my Father had worked there for years 'till he died in 1960. He was a Dray Man and when they took the horses away he went on the wagons. He was never the same man when they took horses away. He died in July 1960; he would have been 61 on the 4th August 1960. When we were kids he would bring hop sacking home from work. My mother would make mats out of them from old coats, skirts and trousers. The hopsacks used to stink like hell.

Brummagem Bill

At work I was delivering catering furniture, drinking glasses and collecting furniture, tables and chairs, to pubs and hotels. Most of the places I went to they would say, "Have a drink driver", "No thanks". We used to have free beer tickets. I was never a beer drinker so I used to put mine behind the bar in a pub at Witton. There was a lot of Ansell's retired men used it so I left them for them. I had to go to a pub in Barnt Green to deliver a safe and bring the old one back. It was up stairs in their bedroom. We got that one down alright but we had a job getting the other one up. We did eventually and the Gaffer said "come on you both deserve a pint". On the way back to Ansell's I started to heave and suddenly I threw up all over the windscreen. I stopped the vehicle, took off my overall coat and cleaned it up. My mate Taffe was heaving up with the smell. I said, "You don't start as well!" It was a summers a day and we had to put up with the smell till we got back to the depot. This sort of thing was going on all the time when you were delivering. If you said "No" they said "what's the matter you can't drink your own beer? I was never a big beer drinker so it was time for me to go.

They was great people there and they all spoke well of my Dad, they used to say he was a jolly type of bloke, always laughing. I said you Surprise me - he was quite miserable when at home.

When Sunday morning came round, he always said roll on Monday morning so he could be back at work. I didn't stay here long, six months at the most. I got a job with Preedy's, the tobacco wholesalers, as a driver covering the West Midlands. Our offices and stores were in Summer Lane, just around from the salutation pub famed for the Brummie song. Nice lot of people worked here, I was one of them. Sometimes I was asked if I would drop some goods off on my way home in my car and I done this on many occasions, I didn't mind.

Chapter Twelve

Whilst we were at Northfield our third daughter, Maryanne was born. I was allowed to see her being born. The midwife always found me a little job to do before, like "let's have a cup of coffee before it all starts". By the time the kettle had boiled and you took it upstairs there would be a baby's cry. "Just a minute Bill", the Midwife would yell out, they had it all weighed up didn't they. Our baby daughter was born on the 28th September 1957 at number 50 Crossland Road, Northfield. Our second son John was born at Selly Oak hospital; Doris had a very bad time delivering the placenta. The placenta came away first creating quite a few problems for them both.

Valerie went to Tinkers farm school and in the senior girls; her headmistress was a Miss Aslin. This was the year 1961, she said to Valerie "Is your fathers name William", and she said "Yes Miss". "Oh, dear" she said "I hope you don't give me any problems, I was his junior teacher at Peckham Road, Kingstanding", I remember her. She used to slap your knuckles with the ruler. I also had my left hand tied to try and make me use my right hand. The teacher was so kind in my days at school! The cane, the slipper, the end of the rope in the gymnasium, I think they must have been a bit on the kinky side. Mind you, it didn't do us any harm. If we went home and told our mothers we would get a good hiding off her as well for not behaving yourself.

Valerie did do better than me; she got in the prizes for her work. I have a book to prove it with her name inside, it is by Norman Bartlam called 'School Days around Tinkers Farm Northfield'. Sadly, the school was demolished in June 2000. The same thing happened to Peckham Road School that I went to, both to build new housing estates on. Where are the children of these new estates going to get their education from?

Valerie and Billy had the chance to go to college; Valerie said she would not wear a Boater or a Joseph Technicolor blazer. And Billy said the same. Your Mother and me thought you would both look nice in them (never mind). My youngest son David, he went to Wolverhampton Technical College and Coventry University, my other daughters Linda and Maryanne and our youngest daughter Pauline I will tell you all later on in the book of their lives.

We moved house to 215 Colonial Road, Bordesley Green. I asked one of my Gaffers if I could loan one of the vans to move some delicate items, glass etc, and the top Gaffer said yes. So when the time came to use the van the other Gaffer said "Hold on", he come over to the van, checked the mileage, how much petrol was in, I told him he could stick the van where the sun don't shine and told him not to ask me again to do any more deliveries in my own car on my own. The other Gaffer could see what was happening and come over, I told him what he said, he said, "Bill, take the van, fill it up with petrol and use it as long as you like". Thanks Gaffer.

About this time, on the 20th May 1963, at 215 Colonial Road Bordesley Green our eldest daughter was working at a builders firm in the office. One of their drivers told her there was a driver's job at Derrington's, Speedwell Road, Hay Mills, another building company. She come home and told me, I went up and took the job on. It was driving a 7-ton tipper truck, delivering sand and gravel cement etc. Derrington's was a big firm and had branches all over the midlands. Their main offices and yard was at lower Dartmouth Street, Bordesley. They had Birmingham and Fazeley canal running in the yard. A lot of their building materials used to come by it. I had to go there from time to time, when our holidays come around there was no holiday pay. I used to go and work casual at Smiths Brewery, Lichfield Road, Aston with my Father in Law Frank. But this occasion I was approached by one of our customers. He had a gang of workers in the Dunlop's on their close there he said he needed more men so I accepted and worked my two weeks holiday. When it was over he said "How would you like to stay on, on permanent" the money was better, so I agreed, I stayed with them for a while.

My son John, his birthday was coming up and I said "what do you want for your birthday?" he was very interested in birds – Canary's and British birds. I knew of several people in the bird world so I made enquiries and a friend of mine who flew pigeons put me in touch with a Canary breeder over at Brownhills. I went over to see him but he did not have any for sale, but he knew someone who was giving it up so I went over to see this chap and bought all his breeding cages off him and equipment plus the birds. That year John joined a bird club and showed some of his birds, he won quite a few cards and rosettes and best novice rosettes!

We had a bit of scare on the 21st November 1974 with the IRA bombing. Our daughter Linda worked at HMV in New Street Birmingham and she had a part time job as a barmaid at the Tavern in the town next to HMV. But luckily she was off duty. That night our other daughter Maryanne was in town, had heard the explosion and was on her way to see Linda but the Police stopped her and told her the road was closed. There was panic everywhere, she came home very upset and shaking, we didn't find out until later that she was off duty that night and thank God for that, but a very scary moment.

In the Birmingham Mail one night the Army emergency reserve was looking for volunteers, two weeks, one a year, with pay. I volunteered, went to Birmingham, passed my medical, my full kit come by post and went on my first camp, Blackdown in Dorset. They asked if any one of us was drivers, I said I was and they said you can be the Co's driver. They made me the Co's driver, I had to pick him up at the officers mess, drive him over to the lines to inspect and on to the training, exercise area, then back to the mess for his lunch, then pick him up later and back n the exercise, till night time.   At the end of two weeks, we was paid and returned home a few weeks later.   My eldest brother Arthur come to see me, I told him about the AER and he said he was in the TA based at Stoney Lane , Sparkbrook he was a SQMS. He was off to Germany for two weeks. He said he got gratuity every year plus pay every month, he was employed there as a store man driver in a civilian capacity and was SQMS on drill days. He says there was a driver's vacancy going there so I took it.

I Joined the TA, Royal Artillery as a driver, collecting stores and taking the 25 pounders guns down to different colleges with a sergeant for him to instruct the young officer cadets as part of their training. After a few months here a vacancy came up for a store man driver at 23rd SAS regiment Thorp Street barracks in Birmingham. I applied for the post, was vetted and got it on the 12th October 1964 and went on several exercises in England, Wales, Scotland and on the continent.   I qualified as a parachutist on the 23rd March 1966 at RAF Abingdon, Oxford. D.Zs was at Weston on the Green, balloon and Beverley aircraft I terminated my engagement on the 11th October 1968. I made SQMS by the time I had finished.

I was selling door bells around Small Heath, the back to back houses and there was these people moving out – Chelmsley Wood had just been built then and people were moving out to it. And this bloke was a lodger there at these peoples house and he's got a 'joey' on his back, a hump, and he'd got this big belt on and he said, "I've got to go, I've got to find somewhere to go, I've got nowhere to go" and he said "I've got to take me piano, that's the only things I've got and thats what I do, I play the piano, I go round to the pubs and play piano. That's the only bit of furniture I've got. "

So I said "look I'll tell you what I'll do, do you like doing a bit of gardening? And washing a few plates up?" So he said "yes" and I said "well you can come and live with me mate". And he said "can I?" and I said "yeah!" And he said "where do you live?" and I said "I live over in Sheldon", I said, "here you are, I'll give you my address" and I said "you come over any time you like and bring your piano with you and just knock on the door and if I'm not there the Wife will let you in". So I gave him the address and then thought no more about it. Anyway, a couple of weeks went by and our Fred he comes to work and he said "you've dropped me right in you have!" I said "Why?" and he said "some bloke turned up", and of course I've forgotten all about it by then, he said "some bloke turned up, bloody big hump on his back, Dolly opened the door and he said, I've come, I've got me piano", and the people had took the piano for him and dropped it off on the pavement! She said, "You've got the wrong house" and he said "No, is this Wintle? Fred Wintle? I've seen him and he said I can move in. And I'm going to do a bit of gardening, do a bit of washing up and he said I can come and bring me piano with me as well". She said "don't you get moving that piano", and he said "where is he?", she sent him up to the pub and he was looking around and he couldn't see me so he went up to the bar and he said "I'm looking for a Mr Wintle" and the barman said there he is sat over there and pointed to our Fred and he said "Are you Mr Wintle? Fred Wintle?" And he said "Yes that's right". And he said well you're not the bloke that said I can come and move in with him, and bring me piano!

I met an old pal who was a Sergeant cook in the regiment told me there was a good job going at his place, Booths Limited, Kits Green Road. My work was very quite at the time so I took it driving, a stacker truck driver and an overhead crane driver on shift work. I done this for about 8 months and left, shift work was not good for me. I got a job at Oldham's batteries, driving around the Midlands. I would do Hereford one day, Northampton, Coventry, Leicester, Black Country, sometimes the potteries and Shrewsbury. The depot was five minutes walk from where I lived at 215 Colonial Road, Bordesley Green. (Oldham's Battery closed down we was all made redundant).

Brummagem Bill

I was racing pigeons at this time so I took them with me and trained them. The four corners of the loft, if the wind was against them, the better. I won at different race points through to Thurso and won, including the Thurso where I was first club and second federation and young birds I flew and won through to Berwick, where I won and topped the federation there. The club I was in was the south Birmingham North Road and the secretary at the time was Bill Hopkins, a gentleman of the sport and the chairman was Knocker Griffiths, the Clock Setter was Bill Lambly. Billy's mother and father used to keep a shop on the Bordesley Green Road selling corn and seeds and pigeons. One of the top flyers at this club was a chap called Alfe Pope he was our RSPCA man, he made us all join the RSPCA. I went with him once down Hay Mills, one of our members had some rats was nesting in an outhouse that was full of rubbish. I took a ferret of mine down there, we emptied the outhouse there was rats running all over the place, there was some waste ground at the back, most of the ran in that direction. I think it was an old brickyard or quarry at one time. We had all put our trouser bottoms into our socks, I don't know who was frightened the most, us or the rats. Good fun was had by all, including the rats that got away.

If a bird come back from a race, with broken legs or ripped open, some fanciers would kill it. I took one back that came in to my loft one day, his name and address was stamped on its wing. I phoned him to say, I was bringing it back to him. His wife answered the door she said, "Would you take it around the back gate", I took it, the chap took it off me and said, come down and have a look at the birds. When I got down to the bottom of his garden he had killed the bird and said, "He won't bother anybody again" and chucked him on top of a few more dead birds.

He started to pick them up one after the other telling me how much he had paid for them. I left him and said if pigeons had that affect on me, I would pack them in. Pigeon fanciers are some of the best people n the world. Like most sports, there are some great characters. I think the pigeon fanciers had the best. One of our club members didn't time in, it was a hard race and he come in to the clubhouse on the night sucking one of his kids dummies. Small things like this added a lot of humour at the club. The north road racing was hard, and some very good birds were lost on it. The south road was better; I raced both and won on both. Some fanciers would beg to differ, my Thurso hen, a blue Marriott hen, was first club Thurso, second fed. Should have been first fed.

The pigeon was walking in the garden when I took my clock down, a couple of years later I sent her to France and timed her in.

My Dad kept chickens during the war; well most people did to help out with food shortage. He bought some chickens off a friend, Kirby's down Miller Street, Aston. I went down with my mate, Tommy Simpson, there was a dozen. We put six in each sack and brought them home on the bus, we would have got prosecuted today but things went on like that during war days. One of the chickens later developed a swelling in one of his gills, my Dad said to me, "Kill him before I come home tonight", the bird was still laying eggs and I thought it's a shame to do that, so I got one of my Dads Gillette razor blades, lanced it open and squeezed it out, it was like a big lump of gristle. I showed my Dad when he come home from work and told him the chicken was OK. The chicken lived for many months later.

When I was racing my pigeons occasionally I would get one back with a broken leg or ripped open through the telegraph wires I'd put the leg in splints and stitched up the bird with cotton. My young daughter at the time Pauline was in the garden when one of my birds came back from one of the races - cut open. I said "Pauline, go and get me a needle and cotton quick" she went in to the house come back out, and said "what colour Dad?", I said the pigeon don't really mind what colour it is, she come back with it and I stitched it up, put it in the hospital nest box and lightly fed him till he had heeled up and raced him the next year.

I remember one year going to the Isle of Wight. I used to be messing around a lot... I'd be asking somebody "excuse me, can you direct me the way to Kingstanding?" And they'd be standing there looking confused and say "where's Kingstanding?" and all Val's kids would be laughing their heads off in the back of the car!

And I said to this one woman, "I've lost me parrot! Have you seen a parrot? There's a thousand pounds reward for it if you can find it. And she asked me what colour was it!!

Chapter Thirteen

Brummagem Bill

A few years ago John Hudson and I went to a beer festival in Belgium at Wieze and then up to Holland to a Dutch Pigeon fancier's loft. There was a show on at their club and the chap we went up to see took us to it. They were very nice people and made us very welcome. Two of their members told us to go round to their loft and pick any pair of pigeons to take back home with us. I chose two from each member's loft. A couple of weeks later, one of the lads from Birmingham who had got an import license, went over and picked them up for me, we stayed at a pub one night, the owner got up in the morning and coked our breakfast for us. He said on the night there's drinks in the fridge, just help yourselves and John Hudson certainly did.

Another night we slept in the car, it was a big car park. We parked up and walked over the road to a pub, we bought ourselves a drink and when we got to the bottom of the glass two more drinks were put at the side of them. It happened the next time with a cigar put at the side of them, it was the boss man himself this time, and we were both flabbergasted. We bought them one back when it was time to go, John and a bloke from England was going up into the Centrum (town centre) I said I'm off to the car and get me head down, I said take your car keys and you let yourself in when you come back.

Daylight come, no sign of John Hudson, and it was the noise of the market stalls being put up all around the car. I got out and one of the Dutch men said, "You'll have to move your car, or the police will impound it", John had go the keys to his car. I went over to the pub we was drinking in to see if he had gone back there, she said he had not. I said, would you phone the police to see if he was looking for his car. She did and they said they don't know of anybody lost.

I went back outside and I spotted a police car coming down the road, I flagged them and I spotted John in the back, grinning all over his face. I said, "Come and get your car out now, they're going to impound it". We got in the car and off. His pockets were full of conkers, he had been walking along the road looking for his car and picking up bloody conkers.

The next time we went to a beer festival it was at Munich, the big one. We took our son John to this one, we had a good tour of Germany and up in the cable car to the top of the mountains. In Munich we parked in the multi story car park. When we was ready to come out John Hudson told our John to lift the barrier up, I said "don't do that, the police will be over, and you are probably on camera" In any case, he did and the alarm went off. Then their security officers came over, they had to pay up.
Later, I sold all my birds and clock and took a rest from them. I

bought myself a wire fox terrier bitch, a pedigree, soaked with champions in her papers. My great uncle, Sid Haines, used to breed those years ago and sell them on. He sold one to some big man in the fox terrier world and he made it a champion, he also done some showing round the local pubs in Birmingham and won several cups. I have a photo of one of his dogs, and the cups he won, I thought, "well, if I am going to have a go at showing like him, I had better join a club" so I joined the fox terrier associations and met some very nice people. A lot more serious types than the pigeon's people. I went to the meetings that was held in Digbeth Birmingham Midland Red club buildings and met some people who lived near me a Mr and Mrs Bob Palmer from Epsom Grove. Their prefix was Brumvilles, named after Birmingham City and Aston Villa. Claude Holmes of Sutton Coldfield, he used to trim my dog and some of the club members. My bitch was Manor Dale Melody bred by Miss S Steele of Stratford upon Avon; I had her as a puppy. When she came in to season, I took it up North with Mr Holmes to be mated to CH Cripsey Captain Poldark. She had a nice litter of pups, I sold one little bitch to a Mr and Mrs Bernard Hadland of Yardley Birmingham. My prefix was Tantaus and the pup I sold to them was Tantaus Royal Lass. They showed her all over England and Wales and it was made champion in 1979 at Birmingham. So I did what my great Uncle did.

Chapter Fourteen

I moved to 192 Cooksey Lane; Kingstanding from Bordesley Green. I met up with some of my old school mates. They were members of the Old Oscott Working Mans Club so I started to go and have a drink down there. After the pups was sold some member was looking for a bitch for breeding, he was a member of the fox terrier association, he lived on the outskirts of Birmingham, had seen the pup that Mr and Mrs B Hadland had bought and liked what he saw. He made me an offer so a deal was made. One Friday night I went down to the club and they were marking the racing pigeons they were racing from the north road. I could feel the excitement in the members as they was putting their birds through, I used to race my birds in the same federation from Bordesley Green.

At this time, I was working for the PDSA, Peoples Dispensary for Sick Animals for a short time. Dyno Rod had started a hygiene side of their business, deep cleaning works canteen, restaurant offices, I was told of this job by my brother in-law. He was a plumber working at Raybones Hockley so I went up to the place, had an interview and they said, "We will let you know". I got it and started work with the manager. He showed me what to do and the high standard of what was expected; I worked with the manager for a couple of weeks and then went with the other two. One was the Foremen, we started to get very busy, they started more people on, and my son was one and later my other son come to work with us. The Foreman got the sack. The Manager come out to see me and offered me the Foreman's position so I took it. We all worked the weekends and late at nights, no social life. My one son went out for drink after finishing work late and on the way back he was stopped by the police, one of the vans rear light bulbs had gone out, they could smell the alcohol on him and he was breathalysed, charged and banned from driving. He worked with me without a van for a couple of months then he packed the job in. We had several people start, but they couldn't put up with the hours and the type of work we was doing - Working with chemicals that you need to work with a rubber mask and rubber gloves most of the time.

Doris, my wife, had got a job nursing at St Margaret's Hospital, Great Barr. She had had been working at Rubery Hospital for over 20 years. She started when we was living at Crossland Road, Northfield when we moved to Bordesley Green she worked at East Birmingham now the Heartlands Hospital but after a while she went back to Rubery Hospital. She liked the type of nursing, that was what she was trained for (Psychiatric) she done 12 hour nights plus the travelling on two buses, plus the walk to the other side of town, so it was a bit much for her. She could catch the PT bus or my son or I would drive her there. St Margret's hospital advertised for staff, she applied and got a job there.   After a few months she told me they wanted more staff on the male side.   She always tried to get me to work in to Nursing but I could not imagine myself doing it, I used to go up to pick Doris up from the hospital from time to time and sit amongst the patients.

I tell you what, it opened my eyes when I went to St Margaret's, which was the longest placed I stayed. And I didn't want to go in. Doris tried to get me to go in there when she was at Rubery and I said "I ain't going in there... Wiping the backsides of people!" And when this started down at St Margaret's, I was working at Dyno-Rod all hours, all hours, you know, seven days a week. We were working Saturday to Sunday.   So you were earning good money but you couldn't spend it!   So what I said is, you have a word with the Gaffer, and she come home in the morning and she said you've got an interview with the head one.   So I went up there and he give me a form and he said fill this in and I filled it in and he said leave it with me the next two or three days and that was it and I had a telephone saying "we're ready when you are". So I had to go up and have chest x-rays, blood tests, to make sure everything was alright and I started.

After a time I got used to them, I felt sorry for some of them. I met some of the charge nurses.   Doris come home one morning and told me they were starting more staff on and asked me to try. I said, "you ask one of the nursing officers first" she did that night and he said, tell him to come up for an interview. I went, met the big man, and filled in my application form waited for a week and I had telephone from the big man saying they were ready when I was. So I gave two weeks notice in, on my last Friday I went in to the office for my wages and was told the Boss had got them he wanted to have a talk to me.   I went home and Doris said, "there was man called earlier on wanted to talk to me" I knew who it was, shortly he come he said" Bill, could we have a talk in the car" I said "Yes" , he tried to keep me working for the company but I just had enough. He said "if it don't work out, come back, I will give you a good reference. I can't give you a bad one" Which I thought was very nice. We shook hands and he left. I had a nice reference sent on to me.   I started on nights at St Margaret's Hospital, they issued me with three white coats, and they took blood samples and chest x-ray. I worked on the wards with mentally handicapped and sub-normal patients.

I stayed here for 11 years. After a couple of weeks, they told me to go and work on the pre-discharge unit they was two houses previously owned by two doctors who worked at the hospital. They had women in the one house and men in the other. We looked after both houses. Doris done one week nights and I would do the following week, we done this for a time and Doris was put on a ward for women on her own.

I was later put on a ward for men, but occasionally I would work on the women's wards, I worked on all the wards on the male side of St Margaret's the majority of the time. I worked on my own, a charge nurse would come round three times a night and do a ward round with you and sign the ward book if there was two of you on duty. One would stay upstairs in the night office and the other one downstairs in the day office. We would start work at 8pm, do a ward round with the charge nurse or sister, discuss anything in the ward report, hand the office keys over and he or she would go home and you would do the same eight in the morning. On the night, at eight, the charge nurse would come to give the drugs out; he had the keys to the drugs trolley. If you was trained you would give out the drugs yourself, I was just a nursing assistant. There were some very violent patients here, they were on medication for it, but they still had their mad moments, I have even had a cup of tea chucked over me!

Brummagem Bill

Up on Barr beacon I rented some land and I kept a couple of calf's a few sheep, chickens and geese and turkeys for Christmas. The sheep had some nice lambs and when they was ready for killing I took then to Walsall Abattoirs with John Hudson, they told me to pick them up the next day. When I did the Manager told me it was a one off and don't bring any more as they only deal with top butchers!

We took them home, got a big piece of ply wood on the floor and John carved them up and put them in the freezers around the family. David couldn't eat any after seeing them running around the field!

Chapter Fifteen

We were both coming up for retirement in the next 18 months and there was a rumour going around for people to take early retirement, we both put in for it and we both got it. We were able to plan our holidays together now we was both working at the same place.

Doris had always wanted to go to Austria, to Salzburg, where the Sound of Music was made, so that's what we did one year and we really enjoyed it. But she would not go up in the cable car, she said she would and bet me £5.00 she would. So we went over to get the ride and I said there's one coming down, she said "where?" I pointed up to it and she got her purse out and offered me the fiver. She said, "I've gone dizzy just looking up at it" So that was the end of that.

We both had a good holiday there, despite not going up in the cable car, we had a good tour round Austria, we went in to Vienna and on our way back we had thunder and forked lighting. It was pitch black. The rain was bouncing off the roads and Doris loved it, she said "it's the Sound of Music weather", it was me this time that was a bit scared and not being too familiar with continental driving.

Another holiday on the continent come a couple of years later, when they took the Berlin Wall down. We went into Colditz Castle and the museum all round the Harz Mountains. I said to Doris, look at all this, and Hitler was not happy with it, he wanted Great Britain as well.

We put our house on the market and on our days off went looking for cottages around Hereford.

We had the Hereford Journal every week and looking for a place we found this mobile home we could have, we went down, took a few things for cooking, and put you up beds and on our days off we spent down there chopping the nettles down that was six feet tall. There was a barn and out buildings for storage. We moved in 3 weeks later, I hired a 3-ton van and some help from my son in law Jon Hudson. We moved in, there was just under 5 acres in front of the house. Later I got a few cows and sheep. Alan Watkins of Wool Hope, used to deliver my hay. The first time I

Brummagem Bill

met him I had a Vauxhall estate with a roof rack on it, I put 20 bales of hay on top. It used to sway from side to side; I had to take the corners very very slowly. From Wool Hope to where our place was they were very narrow lanes and about 2 and a half miles away. I went to Hereford Market every week; Thursday was cattle market and general livestock day. I got my chickens, ducks and two-month-old turkeys, I put the turkey poults up in the loft in the out building to grow and fatten them up for the Christmas Festive. Tony Limb a farmer and Haulier took my cows to Hereford Market and talked me in to having some Dexter cows. They were a rare breed of cows and the meat was of good quality. I bought two off him and his wife Jackie, they are a very nice couple, and they helped me to get started with the Dexter's.

I went over to a place near Tamworth and bought four young heifers and one from a breeder down south. She produced a red calf; it was born on our golden wedding anniversary, so we named her band of gold. Tony and Jackie Limb told me to put in for the small herd competition in our club so I did, it was the Midlands Dexter club and I come second. These Dexter's are all pedigrees; my prefix was Billdor, a part of my name and a part of Doris's. I bred a lovely bull calf, black, Tony kept looking at it every time he come up, he said you should put a halter on him, walk him around, get him quiet for showing. I was not in for that sort of thing all I wanted was a few animals around me.

After a few months, Tony come up and made me an offer for this bull, Billdor Blazeaway. So I sold it to him, it has served cows up and down the country ever since. It was by one of his champion bulls Hector. I eventually sold all of my stock, Doris at the time was not enjoying very good health, and she had to go in to the county hospital in Hereford to have an operation on her bowels. She had a temporary colostomy, she was in the intensive unit for a few days, they took a section of the bowel away and she had to wait until it had healed before they could reverse it. It was a long and heartbreaking time for Doris.

We moved from Little Parlors to Orchard Cottage, a mile away. My daughters and son in laws come over, helped us to move in and decorated from top to bottom. We met our new neighbours Nicky and Jane, they are both stars. We soon become very good pals. If we went away for a weekend there was always a bottle of milk and a vase of flowers on the doorstep and a homemade loaf the following day. To find people like this would be like trying to find a needle in a haystack. After a week, we had a card put on the door from the people up the lane inviting us up there. We went up and met Pauline and Brian, two more very nice people; Champion breeders of the rough Collies, also judges.

Chapter Sixteen

From time to time, our daughters would come over to see us, Linda and Steve come down the one weekend from Lincoln, and on the night, we had a few drinks. At 12 midnight we decided to go to bed, Doris was the first to go up the stairs and she fell on the third stair, we went to her and the skin on her shin had rolled back.

We bandaged it up, she did not want to go to the hospital, and she said she could look after it herself. But it gradually got worse, we went down to the doctors and he said you need to go to Hereford County Hospital for treatment.

They kept her in for a few days and she was transferred to Wordesley Hospital for a skin graft. I was making the journey to Wordesley each day and Pauline said, "Dad, come and stay at our house till Mum goes back to Hereford", so that's what I did.

When she came home, we had to make the journey every other week to the Hereford County Hospital so they could check on it until she was discharged.

She could not climb the stairs so that meant us sleeping downstairs; she was still having trouble with her back.

She has had trouble with back pain for some time and with advancing years it's got worse followed by a bad dose of shingles, small blisters all over her back, coming around one side of her front. She was having a visit every other day from the district nurse.

Doris was having one or two falls a day at this time, one day she fell at the back of the door and I had a job to get in to help her.

Things was not getting any better, one of our daughters Maryanne said why don't you come over near us so we can help out a bit. So Doris and myself talked it over, we loved Hereford and the people nearby but we thought it would be in the best interest for both of us.

So we put the wheels in action and a place came up in Harvington, Evesham. It was a two bedroom bungalow. I hired a Luton van and with the help of John Hudson my son in law and his son Mathew we done a couple of journeys while the rest of my family was sorting out the bungalow. It is a nice spot here, orchards all around us, and ten minutes to Evesham.

We both like Evesham, they have a nice indoor market and just ten minutes is Pershore, another market town. We both booked in with our doctors in Evesham town centre, they're very good and would come out to you if needed which was quite often for Doris.

Sometimes during the night she was finding it very difficult to walk and a walking frame was a task for her to use. She would fall over sideways.

Eventually she went in to Evesham Hospital then on to Worcester, back to Evesham and in to Redditch and back to Evesham. She come home for a short time, we was having a nurse coming in of a night and again in the morning to wash and dress Doris. She was awake most of the night and was asking me to phone the doctors to come and see her.

Doris was taken back in to Evesham hospital, she was later transferred to Worcester Royal, and she had a birthday there.

The nurses come on the ward with a birthday cake and we all sang happy birthday to Doris. This was sadly to be her last one. She went back to Evesham and was put on the ward for very ill people.

And this is where Doris died. A call in the morning from the hospital to me to get up to the hospital as Doris had taken a turn for the worse.
I phoned Pauline and told her, I tried to phone David but he was out at work. He was driving a coach to London for the National Express.

All the family come up to the hospital, she was awake when Pauline and I got there. She asked for a drink of water, eventually she went to sleep.

She was taken to a side ward so we could all be with her. She passed away at five minutes to six on the night on 1st October

2005.   David had just missed her; he had been a constant visitor throughout her illness.   I phoned his works on the morning but it was engaged and I had to get up to the hospital ASAP.

She had been in constant pain from the Osteomyelitis in her spine and joints.
Her hands were just as bad, her fingers were closed on to the palms of her hands.

She would try and push paper tissues between her fingers and the palms of her hands.   It was only a few years ago she was doing crochet, she made some lovely children's shawls for most of our grandchildren and great grandchildren.

Pauline and myself always seemed to be up at the hospital, Doris used to call us, 'the old Faithfull's.   I went up twice a day; Pauline was up most days, and David he has to come up from Birmingham Maryanne come up after work when she could. Linda, she lives up at Lincoln but phoned most nights.   Valerie, she would come over on the train quite a few times at Hereford and sometimes stayed over with me.   When Doris went in to Worcester Royal Pauline stayed overnight a couple of times at the hospital.   She had a chair at the side of Doris's bed.
The nights this happened, Val and John stayed with me in

Evesham and arranged with Pauline that we would go over in the morning and have breakfast in the hospital canteen. Then Pauline would go and have some sleep in the car, we stayed with Doris.

Doris is out of pain now and at rest in a woodlands cemetery at West Hall Park, Holberrow. I have paid for a plot and a hazel tree, any member of our family if they wished can have their remains scattered there too.

Chapter Seventeen

For the next two years and so far this year I have spent most of my weekends at Pauline and Keith's home, and the Christmas and I have had a couple of holidays with them. One in Rome, the next year at Prague, they were fantastic holidays. David & Justin took me on a week's holiday in Cornwall on a campsite at Bodmin. We visited Tintagle and Bude, also the Eden Project. The weather was not very good, we had thunder and lightning the first night. At the end of our holiday we called at Cheddar Gorge on the way back and went down the caves there and bought some cheddar cheese. A good day and a good week.

A couple of weeks after Doris had died I joined a rambling club at Harvington and I have been in it since. We meet up at the village hall, I like walking and I've done quite a bit from time to time. I kitted myself out with all the gear and am enjoying every minute of it. Some of the club members would make their own way to the start of the walk, these walks continue throughout the winter months. We would have a meal at a pub half way through the walk or at the end, arranged by the leader and the pub owner. They are a very nice crowd of people.

In November 2007 Linda and Steve took me over to their place in Spain for the week, the weather was warm but the week previous they had gale force winds along the coast doing a lot of damage to the sea front. Cars had been lifted and smashed into each other. In the afternoons we went up into the mountains to some nice restaurants, on the mornings I would take myself off for a walk down to Calpe beach for a good walk along the sea front. Again all good things must come to an end, we came back home, Pauline and Keith came over to Linda and Steve's and took me back on Sunday.

Christmas was here and Pauline, Keith, Laura, Billy and Peter made sure I was going to spend a second year of Christmas with them. David & Justin would come too. Linda and Steve would come up the week before Christmas at Pauline and Keith's, their Christmas starts the 1st December and goes into mid January. I was going to be 80 on the 7th, frightening ain't it, I can't stop shaking. I just think of that TV programme, 'One Foot in the Grave'. I told Pauline and Keith I did not want any fuss, I know what the pair could get up to. They said there's not going to be any fuss Dad. Good thank God for that. There'll just be us Dad.

Pauline and Keith said we have booked a small cottage up in the lake district for a few days and he produced some paperwork with a cottage on it, but it was for six people not eight, and no dogs was allowed. I phoned Keith and told him, he said he had spoken to the people and got the OK.
The extra persons, I thought he was just keeping quiet about it.

The time come and I went and stayed overnight at Pauline and Keith's house, he was working that day and we was travelling up on the night. Billy, Liz, Peter and Hollie their dog, they went up in the daytime. When Keith came home we loaded up and I passed a remark about all the food in the boot but he just shrugged it off.

Brummagem Bill

It was very dark when we arrived in the area, we drove up and down this road, Billy, Liz and Peter had left Redditch earlier on in the day so Keith phoned Billy on his mobile to get some bearings. I said to Keith, "If you find the church you will not be far", he was not taking any notice of me.

We eventually got there and I thought this is not a small cottage, we went inside. There was a big room with a long table in it, I turned into another room and the game was up. My grand-daughter Debbie, her husband Andy and their little daughter Emily, Don and Elaine and their daughter Claire, Laura and Andrew turned up. Maryanne and Tim brought up Stephen, Debbie's brother and his two sons Tom and Daniel. Debbie and Stephen are my eldest son Billy's. He died in 1991. I wished he was here with his family, he would have been so proud of them, they are all a credit to him and their mother Lynne. I would like to think he and his mother was looking down on us on this special occasion, I love you both.

David and Justin joined us, David is our youngest son, and he has been a rock to me since his Mum died. Frank and Emma from Congleton in Cheshire came up to represent the Williams family, how many more surprises!? And Becky and her friend came over, Becky is Debbie's daughter.

The weather was not too good, it rained a lot, but it did not stop us from going out on some walks. On my birthday we all went down to a pub called the Mason's Arms in a village called Gilcrux not far from the Big White House where we was all staying.

The Big White House was all decorated out with balloons and posters. There was a room with a pool table in it; there was a TV room, a summer house outside for the smokers, a room with a computer in it, a washing machine, tumble dryer, everything you needed. Pauline told me Debbie had organised all this, she took on a very big responsibility, a security and protection against any damage, but I hope everything went OK Debbie? (Thanks a lot Debbie, love you XXX).

The nearest town was a place called Cockermouth for any needed provisions; we visited Keswick, Grasmere, Ullswater, Windermere, Rydall, Ambleside, and Maryport. There was plenty to eat and drink (whiskey galore), I could have stayed here, I've had the most wonderful birthday ever and would like to thank you all who made it up the Big White House, and those who could not make it a very big thank you, I will never forget it, I love the whole lot of you and big kisses all round you are all fantastic.

Keith got the photos developed and put them in an album for me, something to look back on at Keith's small cottage up in the Lake District.

Chapter Eighteen

Things got back to normal, I started my walks again. We was going down to the Cotswold's next week, there was going to be twelve on it and lunch afterwards.

We all had eaten our meal and the owner cleared the table and then come in with a cake with all candles lit up on it and they all sang Happy Birthday to me. A nice surprise - but very embarrassing. I was glad when it was all over. They are a very nice lot of people.

Linda and Steve come down from Lincoln and took me back with them for a week. I had a nice week, a day out to Sandringham, the Royals retreat, a walk in the big house and the museum and the church and a nice meal afterwards. A very nice day out.

On the Saturday Pauline and Keith come up to take me back. The following week we was going back up to the Lake District, couldn't wait.

June 9th, when we got ourselves sorted out at the campsite, we took a two mile walk to the pub and had a roast meal, beef. A couple of drinks and then a walk back to the camp. A couple of more drinks and then to bed. The next morning was to be our first serious walk to Orrest Head, near Lake Windemere. This was Wainright's first ever walk in the Lake District. It was a nice warm day and clear sky; you could see the mountains from miles away. We finished the walk and did some more sightseeing, then back to camp, another walk to the pub for our roast beef – the Yorkshire pudding was a bit scorched. I remarked to Pauline about it, she said the gaffer could hear me, when he come over to collect the plates he apologised for the Yorkshire pudding and put a five pound note on the table. We gave it back when we left – me and my big mouth.

The next day we was going to Ullswater and a boat trip one way and walk back to Pooly Bridge, six miles back and more sightseeing. On the night at the Engine Inn I had a change, fish and chips and enjoyed it. Another nice day out and looking forward to tomorrow, it was Grasmere, Helm Crag. It was a three mile in distance but a climb of 1,229 feet. We climbed the lion and the lamb, Pauline had made some sandwiches so we sat down and had them and started the walk back.

We called in to the Dale Lodge Hotel in Tweedies Bar and had a few drinks, called at Dove Cottage and the museum of William Wordsworth and his sister Dorothy's Place. Then back to the camp site, a wash and a freshen up and it was up to another pub, this time called the Pheasant Inn for our meal, then it was back to the camp site, this was our last night here, all nice things come to an end too soon.

Another lovely day after cleaning up and packing up and loading up, we was already to drive home but Keith and Pauline said they would call in to Kirkby Lonsdale and have a look around, they stayed here some time ago. We had a drink at the place they stayed, a look around the shops and then home.

Epilogue

Brummagem Bill

I spoke to my sister recently and I didn't mention the book to her, and then I phoned me brother Arthur as I hadn't spoke to him in some time and then his wife wanted to come on the phone and have a chat with me. I dropped it out to her that Debbie and David was a coming down. Debbie was coming down from Liverpool and David was coming up from Birmingham and I said that we're going to do this book. She said what book's that?   I told her she said you're not writing a book are you?   Are you going to get it published?   I said no it's too expensive. I'm just going to get some copies done to put around the family.   She was really excited!

This book has been coming for some time; I more or less started it off with my brother in Law Frank. Because Frank turned round and said, "You know, some of the things that you've done in the past?" he said "Bill, you should put all this down on paper and write about it, so you can see it at a later date."
So I just laughed it off, I'm not writing all that stuff down! I mean there's some stuff I daren't write about but then there's other things that would be interesting and because I've got a pretty good memory I thought I'll do a bit. So I've been doing this for quite some times now on and off.   I'll do a bit then leave it then come back to it and do a bit more. Things come back to my mind

a lot at night and then I get out of bed to write it down. Thing is I could be wide awake, I go to bed feeling very tired and as soon as I put my head on the pillow my brain starts thinking about al different thing, things trigger that and so I think I'll get that in the book!

I would like to say at this part of the book, I enjoyed my childhood adventures in the Kingstanding and Birmingham areas, the time we was evacuated and during the war years. There have certainly been a few hiccups on the way but you get over them and plod on. Having a wonderful Wife and soul mate like I had with Doris you just could not go wrong.

I would like to say at this point a very big thank you to my Granddaughter Debbie and Son David for all their help and encouragement without which this book would never have been completed. Also Debbie's Husband Andy and Frank my Brother in Law for kick starting me in to writing this book.

Frank is my Wife's brother. We spent many a happy time with him and his Wife Edith up in Congleton, Cheshire. They have a very nice family, all grown up now but with plenty of offspring and they are every bit as nice as their Mom and Dad.

Brummagem Bill

Thinking of offspring's, we didn't do so bad ourselves. We had four Daughters, three Sons, twenty-six Grandchildren, Fourteen Great-Grandchildren and a Great Great Grandchild with still time for more! I am coming up to my 82nd year so I am very pleased to think I have kept a few more Brummies about.

Debbie, Me and David

14293962R00070

Printed in Great Britain
by Amazon.co.uk, Ltd.,
Marston Gate.